TRAVELS WITH PA

FRED VAN LIEW

Travels With Pa
Copyright © 2025 Fred Van Liew

Aside from brief passages in a published review, no part of this book may be reproduced or transmitted in any form or by any means, electronic or mechanical, including all technologies known or later developed, without written permission from the publisher.

Cover Design: Paul Tarbox and Jennifer Leatherby
Layout and Copyediting: Jennifer Leatherby

For speaking engagements, consulting, and other inquiries, contact
Fred Van Liew at travelswithpa@gmail.com

ISBN, print: 978-0-9962679-2-2
ISBN, ebook: 978-0-9962679-3-9

Printed in the United States of America

ACKNOWLEDGMENTS

This journey began as a dream, a longing whispered from somewhere deep within. But it would not have taken form, nor found its spirit, without those who met me along the way.

To the strangers who became companions, if only for a moment. Whether it was a kind word, a shared meal, an unexpected conversation, or simply a smile exchanged across language and culture, you reminded me of the beauty of our common humanity. You were the teachers I never expected, and your presence left an imprint.

To Jen and my children, whose love is the thread that ties me to the world:, thank you for letting me go so that I could return with a fuller heart and widened eyes. Your understanding and support allowed me to wander far and wide, and to come home changed.

To my grandchildren, each a bright light in my life, you were never far from my thoughts. I carried you with me, across oceans and through silent streets, always imagining the stories I might one day share with you.

And to Pa, my constant companion, my elder self, my inward witness. You turned this into more than a solo adventure. Your gentle company offered quiet humor, perspective, and grace. With you beside me, I was never alone.

To all who walked with me, whether in body or in spirit, thank you for making this journey one of discovery, reflection, and deep connection.

    - Fred Van Liew

CONTENTS

Epigraph	1
Prologue	3
Chapter One – Portugal	7
Chapter Two – Spain	31
Chapter Three – Italy	52
Chapter Four – Greece	81
Chapter Five – Dubai	104
Chapter Six – Nepal	115
Chapter Seven – Malaysia	168
Chapter Eight – Thailand	174
Chapter Nine – Hong Kong	181
Chapter Ten – Taiwan	195
Chapter Eleven – Japan	222
Afterword	299
Postscript	302
About the Authors	307

EPIGRAPH

One's destination is never a place, but a new way of seeing things.
    - Henry Miller

The end is nothing. The road is all.
    - Willa Cather

Once you've got up
from your chair and opened the door,
once you've walked out into the clean air
toward that edge,
and taken the path up high beyond the ordinary,
you have become the privileged and the pilgrim,
the one who will tell the story,
and the one,
coming back from the mountain,
who helped make it.
    - David Whyte

It's a contention of my father's, believing as he does that those who miss the journey miss about all they're going to get, that people become what they pay attention to. Our observations and curiosity, they make and remake us.
    - William Least Heat Moon

How delicious it is to wake up in a place where no one, no one in the world, guesses where you are. Sometimes I have stopped spontaneously in towns along my way only to taste the delight that no living being can imagine me there. How much that added to the lightness of my soul!
    - Rainer Maria Rilke

Be silent and listen: have you recognized your madness and do you admit it? Have you noticed that all your foundations are completely mired in madness?... Madness is not to be despised and not to be feared, but instead you should give it life... What you call knowledge is an attempt to impose something comprehensible on life.
    - Carl Jung

What if you wake up some day and you never got your memoir or novel written; or you didn't go swimming in warm pools and oceans all those years because your thighs were jiggly and you had a nice big comfortable tummy; or you were just so strung out on perfectionism that you forgot to have a big juicy creative life of imagination and radical silliness and staring off into space like when you were a kid? It's going to break your heart. Don't let this happen... Pick a new direction and aim for that. Shoot for the moon.
    - Anne Lamott

PROLOGUE

For as long as I can remember, I've wanted to travel around the world. No one in my family traveled, so I have to think the seed was planted by Jules Verne. Around the world in eighty days was surely the ultimate adventure. After college I hitchhiked a lot, mostly the U.S. and Canada. Later on it was six months in Central America. When family life came, I was fortunate to visit South America a few times, Europe as well, Jordan, Israel, Palestine, even China and Japan. But not since the days of hitchhiking and riding the rails, the days with no one to care for but myself, have I been alone in the world without agendas or obligations. Turning seventy brought home the cold fact that the window of opportunity was closing. Signs of aging creeping in. An eye in need of cataract surgery, an ear in need of an aid, more frequent naps and earlier bedtimes. And there was the voice, whispering: "If not now, then when?"

And the poets:

Sometimes a man stands up during supper
and walks outdoors, and keeps on walking,
because of a church that stands somewhere in the East.
And his children say blessings on him as if he were dead.
And another man, who remains inside his own house,
stays there, inside the dishes and in the glasses,
so that his children have to go far out into the world
toward that same church, which he forgot.
        - Rilke

Travels with Pa

I want to be born again, in exactly the selfsame life,
aware this time from the inside out, and to stand this time
as a beautiful un-worrying witness, living beyond
the need for this or that; some memory always with me
of a ship making its way through lifting water,
the song of the wind, the song of my mother,
my father's disbelieving, expectant face,
and the crowding, merciful voice of the sea at my birth.
    - David Whyte

And, of course, Mark Twain, the quintessential needler of the complacent and the couch jockey:

Twenty years from now you will be more disappointed
by the things you didn't do than by the ones you did.
So throw off the bowlines.
Sail away from the safe harbor.
Catch the trade winds in your sails.
Explore. Dream. Discover.

So here I am, in the Delta terminal at DTW, waiting to board a KLM flight for Amsterdam and then a mid-morning flight tomorrow to Lisbon. From there, the details are sketchy. Though there is some certainty, as visas are still required at times, even for us privileged Americans. What I do know is that my family has given me permission, better yet, they've given me their blessings, to be true to myself as best as possible and to live out a dream. But for their love and support, I wouldn't be sitting here. I won't be alone, however. My great-grandfather, Fred T. Van Liew, will be my traveling companion. I only knew "Pa" after his retire-

Travels with Pa

ment and long after his traveling days were over. He spoke little, but influenced me greatly with his quiet wisdom and dignified manner. He was in his late 80's then. I'd sit beside him, ten years old and thirsty, breathing in his life of integrity and curiosity. Perhaps this journey is pay back for his profound influence on me. Over the next several months, Pa and I will travel from west to east, completing our journey in late spring, flying home from Japan or South Korea, or somewhere thereabout. Feel free to hop aboard. Perhaps our experiences, observations, and conversations will motivate you. If not, maybe Mr. Twain will.

- Fred Van Liew
January 1, 2023

CHAPTER ONE
Portugal

Getting Started

January 3

It's nice traveling with Pa. He's quiet. Wants for nothing. And keeps up, step for step. I wasn't sure how it would be, having last seen him nearly sixty years ago. He's not aged a bit. Seems younger, even. I'm sure as time goes on he'll tell me how it's been. For now, he seems content to follow my lead.

Pa slept all the way to Amsterdam, waking just as we landed. He was delighted to be on the soil of his forefathers. His one regret, he said, was that he never visited the Netherlands. Never even left the states. I've not processed yet how this trip might be for him. But I think he's as excited as I am.

We arrived in Lisbon late yesterday, navigating the airport with little difficulty. Pa was amazed of course. Everything he saw was new. I believe I'll learn much from him about the art of paying attention.

After figuring out the ticket system, we caught the metro and arrived at our place about dinner time. Following a short nap, we hit the streets in search of Portuguese fare, but settled on Vietnamese instead. We were grateful for the simple meal and the conversation with the owner and his son.

It's 9AM. Time to get out the door and visit the city. Time to really get started. Time to take seriously Henry Miller's reminder that one's destination is never a place, "but a new way of seeing things."

Old Lisboa

January 4

You forget about jet lag until you're in it. Usually it's at nighttime when you should be going to bed, like last night. I walked for hours yesterday, pleasantly exhausted by the time we returned to the Lux Residence. It's ideal. Dark. Quiet. A comfortable bed. But it didn't happen. Sleep that is. I turned on the television and surfed. Junk for the most part. Then the Hollywood channel. One movie after another. Three in all. None I'd heard of and little that can be said about them. At 2PM I'd seen enough and gave it a try, but still couldn't sleep.

A week ago I started listening to *Don Quixote - "El ingeniosa hidalgo don Quixote de la Mancha"* in Spanish. I thought it would be good preparation. At nearly forty hours in length, it should serve me well.

Old Lisboa is a delight - its architecture, plazas, outdoor cafes, energy - a winter escape for Scandinavians, the British, and anyone needing a vitamin D boost. It's a city where sea food reigns supreme and pastries are a close second. Yesterday morning I hung with the tourists. Later I wandered the back streets, like you're supposed to do if you want to dip below the surface.

There was the street art - provocative and anonymous. The sand art, anonymous too. And the young French woman in a quiet alley with dreams, perhaps, of gallery exhibits in her future.

End Of The Line

January 5

There is a place between dark and light, dream and day, where an answer is given and the truth is told. Some mornings I'm in that place, grateful to be there. Like yesterday, when the question "where to?" jostled my pillow. It was posed by Pa who'd read Lewis Carroll long before J.K. Rowling came along:

"Begin at the beginning," the King said, "go on till you come to the end, then stop."

I'd intended to return to Old Lisboa, believing I'd only scratched the surface. The King suggested otherwise. So I pored over the Metro map, landing on Telheiras, the end of the green line. When I arrived, I was far from the cobblestone streets, the shops and cafes, performers and foreigners. A quiet neighborhood, pleasant and off the beaten path, I spent much of the day observing everyday life.

The Metro exit was at the edge of a pleasant park, beyond which a community garden waited for spring, and a small dog enclosure waited for the regulars to arrive. Down a narrow road a Catholic church waited for Sunday Mass goers, and schoolgirls shared lunchtime stories on a park bench. Beyond was the town center with its store front businesses, family owned markets and restaurants. It was a difficult decision, but I chose a tiny Japanese restaurant serving char siu bao, a delicious warm bun filled with steamed pork and vegetables.

I would have stayed the afternoon but needed to move on, having made a reservation for the night in Sintra. An hour west of Lisboa by train, I'd been told it was a magical town not to be missed. The journey from Lisboa to Sintra, the end of the line, is its own story.

Encounters

January 6

I had a bit of stomach discomfort yesterday evening so I decided to forego dinner and settle for a quiet place and a cup of tea. Walking the back streets of Sintra, I happened on The Lawrence Hotel - English, at least in name. Surely tea must be on the menu. Greeted at the entrance by an older gentleman, refined in all respects, I shared with him my need. He responded that the restaurant wouldn't open for another hour, but he would see what he could do. Returning a few minutes later with another gentleman, equally refined, who led Pa and me to a pleasant sitting room with a waiting fire. He inquired of my preference. "Green tea", I told him.

A few minutes later, a young woman arrived with a tray, tea pot, and cup. Her name was Amanda, and for the next while she shared her story. From Brazil, Amanda left her family a year earlier in search of experience. Back home, she has a small English language school which she operates virtually. Amanda loves her life in Sintra - the culture, natural beauty, the people. She also has a passion for history and is presently working with the owner on a history of The Lawrence. Her part is to research, turning over any stone that might provide another piece of the puzzle. She told us that The Lawrence is the oldest hotel in Portugal, established by Jane Lawrence in 1764. For years the hotel offered comfort and refinement for those in need of respite and, sometimes, an audience with the King.

As our conversation continued, Amanda shared that she is a cultivator of medicinal herbs, a healer of sorts, and a mystic. People gravitate to her because of her particular gift. In the old days, she confided, she might have been labelled a witch. Returning to our room, I thought about Amanda and the opportunities travel provides for chance encounters. And I thought of Vasco Almeda, who we'd met on the train the day before. Unbeknownst to me, until it was too late, I had boarded the train from Lisbon on the day of a rail strike. At each stop on the way to Sintra, twelve in all, the train became more and more crowded until, it seemed, our car would surely explode. It was in the "standing only" crush that I met Vasco, a young engineering student who hopes to specialize in green energy. Our conversation ranged from offshore wind farms, the Portuguese educational system, his brother's studies in Belgium, his mother's famous jam, and his family's history, dating back to kings and queens.

"Visit the Palace," he said, "where you will find my family's coat of arms in the circle closest to the King's."

When we finally arrived in Sintra, an hour later than anticipated, I was intent on finding the palace, the coat of arms, and Mrs. Almeda's famous jam.

Travels with Pa

The Palace

January 7

Pa was old for a long time before he crossed over. He likes old things. Old photos. Old paintings. Old people. These days, most of his friends are old. And he likes Old buildings. For that reason he asked if we could visit The Palacio Nacional de Sintra, the palace the young engineer had spoken to us about. On our way to breakfast we walked by the palace. Mid-day, after the clouds had lifted, we returned, stopping near the entrance to observe a young man deep in thought. A painter, it appeared he was studying the two conical structures rising up from the massive complex. Not wanting to intrude, we waited. After a while, and at Pa's prompting, I asked about the tall white "dunce caps".

"They're chimneys," the young man said in a careful English. "For centuries they served the King's kitchen."

He proceeded to share his fascination for the palace and its history, explaining that it was constructed on the site of a Moorish castle destroyed in 1415 to make way for the existing structure. For five hundred years it served as a royal home where, an Islamic artistic style, known as Mudéjar, co-exists with the Gothic-Renaissance style. After offering our thanks, we made our way inside, moving slowly from one impressive room to the other. Intricate Moorish tile complemented European paintings and tapestries. Pa, a lawyer by training, regretted that he'd never studied medieval art or architecture. I admitted that I'd been remiss as well.

Of all the rooms, the one most fascinating, was the "Heraldic

Travels with Pa

Hall" where King Manuel had his coat of arms placed in the center of the room's dome. His message was, that as King, he was the center and top of a society that was both hierarchical and interdependent. Manuel recognized that his power was dependent on the support of the nobility and the nobility obtained its social status from the King. For that reason the nobility is represented by the coats of arms of the 72 most important families. Try as we might, neither Pa nor I could identify the coat of arms of Vasco Almeda's family.

Forsaking our search, we focused our attention on a young woman high up on a scaffold. With pain staking exactness, she applied a mixture of paint and plaster, bringing to life the century old reliefs.

Moving on, we visited the Royal Kitchen then made our way outside, wandering the paths of the garden where royal children had played. Fascinating as it was, we grew weary and returned to the Lawrence in time for High Tea, anticipating black tea and cookies. Carlos, one of the two refined gentlemen from the day before, disabused us of the notion, serving an incredible selection of sandwiches, fried prawns, spring rolls, French cookies - the name of which I forget - and other sweets, accompanied by juice, and tea of course. Foregoing an evening meal, we walked until sunset.

Travels with Pa

The Train To Obidos

January 8

"I believe she's Dutch," Pa whispered, regarding a young woman on our morning walk.

It's interesting how Pa communicates. I recently watched a British spy film. The secret agent stayed in contact with Control with the aid of a receiver hidden in his ear canal. It's like that.

Pa was right. Marga, a recent Harvard grad, will soon return to Amsterdam to begin her new life as an urban planner. In the distance of a block or two, she shared her passion for the proper design of city streets:

Streets are outdoor rooms. They need edges to hold them. They need the texture of trees, fences, gates, walls, windows and doors. They need to be read and understood by people walking through those rooms.

As we parted company, Marga encouraged us to visit Obidos:

It's a perfect example of a town whose streets are outdoor rooms.

And just like that, we changed our plans. Returning to our room, we Googled *Obidos*, studied our map of Portugal, and the train schedule from Sintra to Porto. By noon we were on our way.

I love trains. My father was a railroad man. I rode on an engine almost as early as I rode a bike. After high school, I worked on the rails that transported them. After college I rode in boxcars that rode the rails.

The trains in Portugal look considerably different from those of my youth, but the experience is the same - the sound of metal on metal, the rocking back and forth, the spaciousness, the view, the ease of movement. Pa's experience was different. His father was a coal miner. As a lawyer, Pa rarely left town and either walked or took the trolley to the office. Nevertheless, he took great pleasure in our journey.

We passed vineyards and wind turbines. Stations abandoned and not. Villages, towns and ball fields. The time went quickly and in two hours we'd arrived, the station unoccupied and in the middle of nowhere. We'd failed to consider that Obidos was a thriving community long before trains arrived. Built on a hill, access by rail was never considered. But the walk was pleasant and by the time we'd reached Cafe de Filipes at the base of the fortified town, we were in the best of spirits.

The Magic Of Water And Light

January 9

Obidos at night is magical, even in the rain. And Marga was right, at their best, streets are outdoor rooms. The medieval "Obidosians", if that's what they were ever called, certainly knew that, and planned accordingly. Buildings and trees, walls and doors, hug the hand laid stones that allowed passage by foot and horse drawn wagon. Vehicles aren't allowed within the walls and arched entries provide both access and cover as pedestrians move from one "room" to the next. Lanterns are hung to illuminate so as not to inhibit the display of shadow and shape. Magic requires sleight of hand. There must be limits to what is seen and known.

It's been only a week, but Pa has been transported, back to medieval Utrecht, where his ancestors lived in step with the seasons and the celestial lights of day and night. Utrecht has changed considerably, now a municipality of nearly 400,000. Obidos not so, enclosure limiting its growth to little more than 4,000, residents and tourists the beneficiaries. We could have walked until midnight, but our tiny room beckoned. A good night's sleep is required for exploration.

A Morning Walk

January 10

A cock crowed shortly before 6:00, though the sun would not rise for another two hours. But when it did, an Obidos that invited exploration was revealed, and we were out. There are the churches of course. Aging gracefully to inform the traveler of the faith that once directed the lives of the locals. The dwellings that still house. The bakery that feeds; the bookstore that educates; the pharmacy that heals. But climb above the main thoroughfare, above the side streets and alleys, and you'll find the Obidos that the nesting birds - the harrier, red kite, and wryneck - know best. It's from these heightened places where one can best appreciate the beauty of Obidos and the surrounding countryside that has its own history. But as with all transcendent experiences, one must come down, and eat. Descending, we discovered a delightful side street restaurant serving a salty, garlicky, lemony, baked cod, prepared as only the Portuguese can be.

Obidos

January 11

Obidos is a destination for historians and scholars, poets and painters; for those who visit long enough to relinquish their cares, sharpen their minds and enrich their souls. But there are also many who make their livings within its walls, raise their families outside them, and bury their loved ones nearby. Some were born here, left for Lisbon and beyond, only to return. Some never left at all. And others arrived late in life and for the first time, seeking to escape the weather, the economy, perhaps a past life. Like the couple I met this morning from New Jersey.

Obidos is more than a relic, a living museum, or a stopping place between Lisbon and Porto. It's a place of people, present and past ... like the proprietor, the waiter, the vendor, the merchant, the artisan, the librarian, the stone layer, the chef, the barista, the baker, the bookseller, the supplicant. The dead too. Óbidos is a place where women sing in the street and young people kick up their heels.

Moving On

January 12

Travel, at least on the scale upon which we've embarked, is no different than life day to day, except in degree. Life is compressed, compacted. The lack of routine lends itself to novelty. The morning walk is revelatory and will never happen again. The chance conversation more engaging and will never repeat itself. The Taoists know this, and encourage us as such, but habit is a powerful sedative, numbing our senses and our perceptions.

Three days in Obidos was a week, a month. Each day a seven course meal to be savored for a lifetime. So why leave? Life goes on, of course. There are many more meals and walks and conversations to come. And to remain would close the door on the new and unexpected. So I purchased a ticket for Peniche, 26 km to the west, solely for the way its knob of a peninsula thrusts out into the Atlantic.

Distances by bus can be deceiving, especially when it's a local - stopping for a mother with child, school children, the elderly. But the hour went quickly as there was much to see. By noon we arrived in the town center, in the rain and without directions. Admittedly, I was a bit dejected. Then the whisper:

"Look around young man. All you need is right here."

Pa was right, of course. And look around we did. Across the street and down a bit was O Sebastiao's. Seated, within minutes we were served fried calamari, "smashed potatoes", bread with olive oil, and a glass of the house wine. Life is good.

Peniche is rough around the edges, gritty even. Far removed from the charm of Sintra and Obidos, it has its own history. Long renowned as a center for lacemaking, its working harbor, and the military fortress that kept the English Armada at bay and then Napoleon, pensioners retire here for its affordable housing, easy living, and end of the day tranquility.

Travels with Pa

Little Venice

January 13

We had hoped to visit Porto, the 2nd largest city in Portugal and gateway to the Douro Valley. But recent torrential rains and subsequent flooding forced a change in plans. Instead, we've stopped in Aveiro, a peasant city in the center of the country, self-described as the *Little Venice of Portugal*. The nickname is apt as canals crisscross the town and *moliceiros* ply their waters. Having promised not to scrimp, I gladly paid the 12 euros for an hour with Bruno - skipper, amateur historian, and all around nice guy. Though not his only passengers, it appeared we were the only English speaking ones. Nevertheless, he devoted equal time to our experience. Early in our voyage, Bruno pointed out the sights that line the canals. He spoke of his love of soccer, Portugal's hosting of the 2004 World Cup, the devastating 1-0 loss to Greece in the final, and the country's most recent World Cup loss to Morocco.

"But in the end," he said, "it's only a game. I have a family to support. Family comes before any pastime, no matter one's passion for it."

I told him I understood, deciding not to share my lifelong love for the Yankees. Bruno then shifted the conversation to ancient times when the medieval town was a center of salt mining by the Romans and a trade center for the precious commodity. While the gathering and processing of salt is no longer the primary source of Aveiro's prosperity, harvesting continues to this day. Navigate the canals or walk them, you'll find tribute in art, mural, and sculpture to those whose efforts made it possible for others to season their food, preserve it, or utilize the essential mineral in so many ways.

Sarah And Karen

January 14

It's the side streets that often attract. After the boats and canals, after Bruno and the history lesson, we happened upon an out of the way restaurant, a little place with just a few tables. The smell of garlic, olive oil, and herbs permeated the intimate space, and an open kitchen presented a friendly face. It's Sarah and Lionel's place, hard earned after years in an office for Lionel and the back kitchens of fine restaurants for Sarah. The couple moved in a year ago, hoping for a simpler life, one in which they could set the hours and call the shots. It's working out. They're happier, spending more time with their children, meeting new friend and, for Sarah, creating new dishes her mother would appreciate.

Sarah and Lionel are vegan.

"Meat murders," says Sarah. "It's mushrooms that make the dish and will save the planet."

After an incredible meal of shitake alheira with fresh vegetables lingering in sweet chili sauce, Sarah sat down as Lionel cleaned up. Born in 1974, the year of the "peaceful revolution", Sarah is widely read and well informed, with opinions that support her liberal leanings. She knows all about Trump, January 6, the overturning of Roe v. Wade, and the ongoing threats to democracy. She's disturbed about the direction our country is going, but hopeful.

"It's America", she said.

We spoke about Portuguese politics, the battle for abortion rights, green energy, the decriminalization of drugs and the emphasis on rehabilitation. And, most recently, the Death with Dignity debate. Congress has approved progressive legislation. The president won't sign it. The courts must now decide. Sarah is unsure of the outcome,

"But it's the right thing."

Shortly after returning to our room, an email arrived from a friend in Maine. Karen was a teacher, mentor of the young, fierce advocate for survivors of domestic violence, writer, artist, shamanista, lover of the natural world, believer that death and dignity should be inseparable, and a dear friend. I could write more about Karen. Instead, I'll share her email which she gave me permission to do.

Hello, my Dear Friend,

I have sad news.

The risk of staying has outweighed the quality of staying. Infection and organ failure are too close, and I thought why the heck would I stick around for some horrendous end when I can peacefully go. Today at Noon the doctor arrives. Usually people can drink the medication alone, but my tricky system needs some special care. Donna, Bruce, Pam, and Charlie will be here for the dying. Ali is not coming due to her early pregnancy and because it is so damn hard saying goodbye. People are invited over after I've passed to see me or just support Charlie. The Shamanistas are going to clear the space after the funeral home takes my body. It's been a long haul and I'm ready to give up this body. Friends are filling the house with flowers. I will leave my bedroom garden filled with white flowers. I imagine leaving from the crown. I love you and am grateful for our years of connection. You've been a good friend, teacher, and fellow traveler. I lived vicariously through your adventures and accomplishments. If not for my cancer, I believe I would have followed your example of writing and contemplating through my retirement. It is painful to leave our relationship that feels like there is so much more to talk about.

Be well and continue your wonderful adventures with openness and love.

Goodbye

Lots and Lots of Love,

Karen

Pa sat with me as I processed, providing solace as best he could.

"Death isn't the greatest loss in life," he said quietly. "The greatest loss is what dies inside us while we live."

Karen suffered many losses in her life. The death of soul was not one of them. She moved on at 2PM, survived by her friend and partner, Charlie.

After Dark

January 15

A friend reached out. Touched by Karen's story, she wrote:

"I still have a lump in my throat." I understood.

I walked much of yesterday. Not for new experience, but to connect. In the evening, at the time when we normally prepare for bed, we went out. As everyone knows, Europeans, particularly in the south, are night people. Lisbon is no different. It may, in fact, have written the book on life beginning after dark.

It was a short metro to the Old Town. Sunset passed, a different light marked the way. Ascending a narrow stairway, we emerged onto a quiet street, a lone cafe offered outside seating. The evening's special was written on a chalkboard adjacent to the entry - *creamed broccoli and potato soup*. As one does after breaking a fast, I moved slowly, savoring the soup, the bread, the wine, each complementary.

A young couple seated next to us engaged in small talk, getting to know each other. I thought of Karen and Charlie, their first conversations, and their last. After a while, the young couple left and Pa and I were alone.

Moving on, a bookstore caught my eye and we entered. There were old classics, and many others, telling stories I'll never know. A young woman approached and we talked about poetry. She handed me a slim volume, English on the left, Portuguese on the right. I asked if I could tell her a story. Deferential, she consented.

I was fifty, or thereabouts, studying Spanish for two weeks in a small Peruvian town. On an afternoon I happened on a school for girls. Entering, I inquired if I might observe a class. Soon, I was in front of about twenty girls, white blouses and blue jumpers. At some risk, I thought, I opened my slim volume of love poems penned by Pablo Neruda. English on the left, Spanish on the right. I read one poem, then another, in Spanish. Looking up, I saw how each girl had been moved, gazing in rapture, wiping their eyes. With some hesitation, I turned back toward the old nun. She was wiping her eyes as well.

The young bookseller thanked me, took my hand warmly, then wiped her eyes. We moved on, entering one restaurant then another, wanting to connect. There was laughter, intimacy, connection all about. Midnight neared and we made our way to the Metro, stopping to honor a young musician playing the theme to Dr. Zhivago. I was transported back to the final scene - the old doctor on the train recognizes Laura, passing by on the street. Unable to connect, he watches as she passes by, unaware of his gaze.

I think of Karen, her new life, and Charlie, with a lump in his throat. Daily, I receive an email, a poem or reading, from the pastor of the Unitarian Church of All Souls in Manhattan. I imagine Karen speaking to Charlie as I read Elizabeth Barrett Browning:

If thou must love me, let it be for nought,

except for love's sake only.

Do not say "I love her for her smile, her look,

her way of speaking gently,

a trick of thought that falls in well with mine."

For these things in themselves, Beloved,

may be changed, or change for thee …

But love me for love's sake,

that evermore thou may'st love on,

through love's eternity.

Art As Autobiography

January 16

I wanted to visit the Gulbenkian. Pa resisted. I explained that the Gulbenkian is one of the finest art museums in the world. He responded that he'd not grown up with art and felt ignorant when in the company of those who had. I promised we wouldn't stay long, devoting attention only to what attracted him. He apologized for his reluctance and said he would do his best to appreciate the experience.

Arriving just as it opened, we made our way through the spacious entry, pausing briefly at the welcoming sculpture. I could sense Pa's uneasiness.

"We Dutch are open minded," he said. "Nevertheless, we value proper attire."

I saw no reason to engage him on the subject. After purchasing our ticket, half price with the senior discount, we proceeded to the Egyptian exhibit. Passing quickly by the pottery and metal work, we stopped to admire two male figures.

"They're quite life like," Pa observed, "given their age."

The Islamic exhibit followed. We spent little time with the artifacts. Instead, the figure of a wise old man caught Pa's eye, and the books. As a boy, when he wasn't playing football or baseball, Pa read. He was fascinated by history, geography, and the stories of the great explorers. Though he knows little of Islamic tradition and culture, it somehow resonates with him.

Next, the Far East and a large multi-paneled depiction of medieval Japanese life. Pa studied it for the longest while, particularly the scenes of public areas - the buildings, walls, courtyards. Years before I knew him, Pa had engaged in city planning, having written two books on the subject. Pa then pointed to an older gentleman tending to a child.

"I like that," he said, with a smile.

After Japan, the Renaissance, and paintings depicting New Testament events, I sensed a shift. Pa no longer saw the elaborately framed works as art, but rather as living images, distillations of the stories of his youth. The same with portraits, in which he saw himself as a boy, interested in the way things work. He saw his beloved Bea as she was when they were courting. And as his wife, years later, mother of their three daughters. Then he saw her again, near the end of her life, returning after what had been a very long journey. I asked him how he felt, seeing her for the last time. He answered softly, almost with reverence,

"Death is the cry of a child being called home at dusk."

We spoke little after that, until lunch called. Deferring to Pa, I ordered the quiche.

"Now that's art," he said with a grin.

Public Spaces

January 17

Pa entered the law to avoid the coal mines and the tedium of his father's life. It suited him well, given his easy way with people and penchant for solving problems. Within a few years of earning his license he was well established, making a decent living and supporting his young family. As time went on, his client base grew, as did his areas of interest. He felt especially drawn to public life and public works, and the needs of the larger community.

Travels with Pa

When I asked Pa how he'd like to spend the day, he said he wanted to explore the public spaces where people congregate away from work and home. So we did, beginning with the subterranean. Riding the escalator, Pa was awestruck by the design, engineering and labor that went into the elaborate underground system. But soon enough the art caught his eye. The mosaics and tile work; the life size figures. It pleased him that they were available to everyone, not just the patrons of the Gulbenkian.

Once we arrived at the old city, the streets drew his attention - how they delight the eye, and at the same time accommodate the needs of pedestrians and public transport. After some time we happened on a large plaza which both delighted and disturbed Pa. He liked its vastness but the monument to the victor of some past war was unsettling. So we moved on to the waterfront and the welcoming space leading up to it. As the afternoon waned, we found ourselves in a different neighborhood and a different space where friends congregate and pigeons come home to roost.

You Never Know

January 18

I couldn't recall why we'd chosen to visit Faro. Neither could Pa. We knew nothing of it, except that it's about as far south as you can go before reaching the Mediterranean and then Morocco. But the ticket was cheap and the bus from Faro to Seville inexpensive. And besides, we'd never know what's there without going.

Travels with Pa

We found out soon enough, judging by the station, that it's a simpler place than Lisbon. After a couple of false starts, it was a short walk to the Casa Algarbe where Patricia greeted us, a pleasant woman who took great patience with our limited Portuguese. We settled in, took a short nap, then headed out.

Faro is an old city. Colonized by the Phoenicians in the fourth century BC, the Romans took over 600 years later, giving way to the Byzantines, followed by the Visigoths. The Moors arrived in the eighth century, ruling for nearly 500 years. A lot happened after that but, somewhere along the line, the invaders and colonists lost interest and Faro declined. Now it's a pleasant seaside town where the locals cater to snowbirds and life is slow.

As with any walk without a deadline, you just begin. The Casa Algarbe is on a narrow street that opens onto a broader one, which eventually intersects with the harbor. Moving along, we came upon the sea at low tide, and lingered. With sunset approaching, we took a right and followed the tracks, hoping to re-enter beyond the commercial district. So we set foot on a narrow street which led to another, which opened on to a charming plaza. Beyond, side street after side street led to a second plaza. Had we not found it, we would not have known that D. Afonso III was a benevolent ruler a thousand years ago. That more recently, the artist Isolino Vaz created works to expose the harshness of an unfair society. Or that, between the two, Columbus passed by Faro on March 14, 1493, after leaving Lisbon the day before.

Continuing, there was an old bell tower, on the other side of which, an orange tree. We sat, the lyrics of an old Moody Blues song rising:

Travels with Pa

After he had journeyed,
and his feet were sore,
and he was tired,
he came upon an orange grove
and he rested.
And he lay in the cool,
and while he rested,
he took to himself an orange
and tasted it,
and it was good …

CHAPTER TWO

Spain

Eat, Pray, Love

January 19

If there's one thing I've learned from traveling, especially overseas, it's never to eat or drink prior to a long bus ride. I learned the hard way on a ten hour journey from Guatemala City to the northern mountains. There was no bathroom and only a possible stop. No promise, however, as to when that might occur.

Our bus to Seville was the coach type, operated by *Rede Expressos*, and scheduled to depart at 10AM. That meant nothing after 6:00 the evening before, with the exception of pill taking and teeth brushing.

Though I travel with an emergency device, there would be no opportunity for its use as every seat was taken. Seated to my right was an American woman. Distrustful, she chose not to store her two large bags in the hold below. Instead, she placed one at her feet and the second on her lap, depriving me of a fair share of my allotted space. Without a word, we were off to a rough start.

Fortunately, there was good conversation coming from the seats directly behind. A woman hailing from Queensland, about my age, exchanged travel stories with a Hamburg native. They could have been mother and daughter. The older of the two has traveled widely, outlasting her husband by a decade. She could have been the Rick Steves from Down Under.

I particularly enjoyed listening to the young woman. Married shortly after Obama took office, she travels on her own every year for a month.

"I need a regular dose of solitude," she said. "Plus, it keeps our marriage alive."

Her husband tends to matters in her absence, traveling on his own six months later. She said that ten months together and two months apart is about the right balance, although she has dreams of an around the world backpack trip someday. The Aussie encouraged her without hesitation.

"You must do it dear. Life is so short."

Just as we crossed the Guadiana River separating Portugal from Spain, I heard snoring to my right. My American seat mate was lost in dreams of her own, a well-worn copy of *Eat Pray Love* resting precariously on her belongings. Nearly two hours passed before she woke, just as we crossed the Guadalquivir River flowing through the heart of Seville.

A Time For Beauty

January 20

We're staying at the Hostal Jentoft. Pleasant enough place. Near the bus station and the river, it's on a quiet street within walking distance of the places I've been told we must see. We ate breakfast early and alone, but for the young woman in charge. Quiet, she kept to herself behind the large window, emerging only when necessary. This morning a most beautiful orchestral piece, Bach I think, wafted softly from her private space.

After coffee, toast with jam and yogurt, I spoke with the gentleman at the front desk. He keeps to himself but is helpful when a need arises. At the risk of intruding, I inquired as to where he goes when his morning shift is over and before his evening return.

"Often," he said, in a cultured English, "I visit the *Bellas Artes De Sevilla*, the museum. It's a refuge. A place of beauty."

Pa and I were on the street by 9:00, intending to arrive at the *Catedral De Sevilla* well before its opening. Approaching from a side street, we toured its perimeter.

Raised Catholic, I attended Catholic schools all the way through college. In 7th and 8th grades, I was captain of the altar boys at St. John's Basilica. I learned about kindness from the nuns, and Latin sufficient to make it through the Mass. And something about reverence, silence, even beauty.

Then high school where the priests took over. Judgment and critical thinking slowly replaced the compliant learning of the schoolboy. The process accelerated at the university where the Jesuits insisted that "learning to think" is paramount. By the time I graduated I was a card carrying agnostic.

So we entered the *Catedral*, and into that space that only the architects of centuries ago knew how to create. Their intention at the time, and for the eternity to follow, was to elevate the souls of the faithful, creating a bridge between their mundane lives and their Creator. For most, that's no longer possible. Nevertheless, at least for the time one remains within the space, it's possible to wind back the clock, to suspend all judgment and critical thinking, and be reminded that there is a time and place for reverence, for silence, and for beauty.

I was introduced in Lisbon to the writer, poet, and essayist Fernando Pessoa. Though he lived a relatively short time, 1888 - 1935, he's still considered the foremost Portuguese modernist. I purchased his most acclaimed work, *The Book of Disquiet*, in which he wrote about faith:

I was born in a time when the majority of young people had lost faith in God, for the same reason their elders had it without knowing why. And since the human spirit naturally tends to make judgements based on feeling instead of reason, most of these young people chose Humanity to replace God. I, however, am the sort of person who is always on the fringe of what he belongs to, seeing not only the multitude he's a part of but also the wide-open spaces around it ...

I feel, even grieve for the many young, and not so, who nowhere in their lives are touched by reverence, by silence, by beauty.

New Things And Old

January 21

I met a young man at the Hostal. Just finished with college, he'll fly to Boston in a week to begin work at a homeless shelter following his Gap Year in Nepal. Pa and I will be there in March so we had a connection.

Somehow we got to talking about maps. Turns out his father is an engineer, and a cartographer. Shortly before COVID, his father and three colleagues began work on a navigation app. It's completed, in the App Store, and now on my phone.

"It's better than Google Maps," the young man told me. "Great for overseas if you don't have a SIM card. You can go offline with it."

We set out. Our destination, the *Alcazar*, a royal palace built for King Pedro I of Castile. Arrival at 8:40. I'd been told the *Alcazar* is near the *Catedral* so I had a general idea where we were going. Still, as I like new things, I put trust in the new app as my primary resource. Though the route was different from the day before, I appreciated the change in scenery. 8:40 came. The app said we were close. But we weren't. My trust began to wane. One side street after another. 8:50. No *Alcazar*. I turned off the app and began to ask directions, the old fashioned way. Somehow we got there, just a block beyond the Catedral. I consulted my watch (an inheritance from Pa) its hour hand at 9 and minute hand at 12. Just in time for our ticketed entry. Pa chided me, in a gentle way.

"Young man, you should rely on your watch. It never failed me."

I agreed, not mentioning that it hadn't come with a map.

Some historians date the construction of the *Alcazar* as 1360 or thereabouts, but that's not quite right. It has a much longer history. In the early 900's the caliph of Al-Andalus (the southern region of Spain is still known as Andalusia) built a fortress to replace a Christian basilica. Over the centuries, various demolitions, constructions and expansions took place resulting in a massive complex. When the Christians again took over Seville, the *Alcazar* was converted into a residence for the monarchs. King Pedro's people modified it, the result being much of what is seen today.

Entering the *Alcazar*, we were transported and, after a slow, contemplative afternoon, we were on the streets again, where we found an old fashioned map to guide us. Our day ended at the Casa Placido followed by a restful sleep.

Today, however, I walk with a heavy heart, having learned of David Crosby's passing. I'm transported to the olden days when music was my guiding star.

If you smile at me I will understand

'Cause that is something

Everybody everywhere does in the same language …

¿Que Es Este Lugar?

January 22

There is a point with travel when you cross over. I suppose it's different for different people. For me, it's happened twice. When I hitchhiked after college and again, five years later, when I spent six months in Central America. And now a third time. It's that point where you cease to be a tourist and traveling becomes what you do. In the past, one may have been a pilgrim, the pilgrim

Travels with Pa

type without a destination.

The poet David Whyte knew:

Once you've got up

from your chair and opened the door,

once you've walked out into the clean air

toward that edge,

and taken the path up high beyond the ordinary,

you have become the privileged and the pilgrim,

the one who will tell the story …

Today is the twenty-first day. Perhaps I'm on the cusp of it. It's a fascinating place. A different reality. One in which, as Lewis Carroll wrote, the unexpected is to be expected.

Either the well was very deep,

or she fell very slowly,

for she had plenty of time

as she went down to look about her

and to wonder what was going to happen next.

Yesterday we visited the *Mezquita de Cordoba* - the *Mosque of Cordoba*. And if you're Christian, the *Mezquita-Catedral de Cordoba*, perhaps more suggestive of its history. I knew little of it, and Pa nothing at all. At night, and from a distance, it's a heavenly site on a hill above the city. During the day and up close, you can barely grasp its immensity. But at some point you must enter, and be confronted with the unexpected. And the utterly unexpected is what you find.

There are few words in our language to express it, to describe its other reality. At first, and for quite some time, one can only wander, and ask:

"What is this place, a maze, a puzzle? Is it a dream?"

Time does not exist within the walls of the *Mezquita* so it's impossible to say when the shift occurs, when the eyes begin to focus and more questions arise:

"But on what? The columns? The arches? The paintings? The statuary? The light?"

We stayed until hunger demanded our attention. Finding a resting place, there were more questions:

"Who were those people, those architects of the sublime? Were they aliens? Residents of an advanced civilization?"

We tried to place ourselves in their company and felt very small.

No Strangers Here

January 23

The American short-story writer Washington Irving (*Rip Van Winkle*, *The Legend of Sleepy Hollow*) visited the Andalusia in the spring of 1829. In recounting his journey from Cordoba to

Travels with Pa

Granada, he wrote:

The dangers of the road produce a mode of traveling, resembling, on a diminutive scale, the caravans of the east. The arrieros, or carriers, congregate in convoys, and set off in large and well-armed trains on appointed days; while additional travelers swell their number, and contribute to their strength. In this primitive way is the commerce of the country carried on.

Pa and I saw nothing of the sort yesterday, traveling as we were at 185 mph. Perhaps caravans are still there, off in the distance. But if not, one can imagine, as arid deserts, fertile plains, and plantations of subtropical fruits still dominate the landscape.

There are certainly differences. The small, multi-colored homes now sprout antennas from their roof tops. Roadways, narrow and wide, are populated with modern, four-wheeled carriers. And commerce is carried on as much by smart phones as by convoys. But step off the train in Granada, and the sight is the same now as it was for Mr. Irving nearly two hundred years ago. At one time, Granada was known in Arabic as *Gárnata*- "the hill of strangers."

On our thirty minute walk from the station to the *Palacio de los Navas Hotel* we witnessed nothing like that but, instead, observed friends congregating and dining together; couples walking hand in hand; young people "chilling," and infants strolling. Come five o'clock and the streets were empty. But by seven they'd come to life again.

Tomorrow we'll visit the *Alhambra*. Having read something of Mr. Irving's account, we're hopeful nothing has changed. But if so, we will imagine.

What Is Heaven Anyway?

January 24

Today was the day, the *Alhambra*. At breakfast, I shared my excitement with Pa. He didn't respond at first but then, somewhat sheepishly, asked if he might stay behind. Travel had left him fatigued.

"I'm in need of rest," he said.

"Of course," I told him, promising to give him a full report.

The *Alhambra*, being the once in a lifetime experience that it is, requires planning. Watching a good YouTube or two. Reading Mr. Irving's *Tales From Al Hambra*. And getting a ticket in advance. The entirety of the *Alhambra* is worthy of one's complete attention, but the Nasrid Palaces especially so. The timed entry was for the Nasrid. To be late is to forfeit your right to entry. So I purchased my ticket for 1PM, arriving at the entrance to the complex shortly after 10:00. I wanted plenty of time to prepare.

Wandering about, looking, lost in my thoughts, I found myself with my grandchildren some years from now. It was a holiday and all seven had made it. They were gathered around and the questions began. A hand went up. It could have been any of the seven as they're all good students.

"Papa, tell us about traveling. About Portugal and Spain. About the *Alhambra*."

And so I did. I told them that many books have been written about it, the most famous by Mr. Irving. Of course they all knew of him having read *Rip Van Winkle*.

"To visit the *Alhambra* is to visit one of the most famous monuments of Islamic architecture. Some say, the most famous. Work was begun in 1238 by the Nasrid ruler who founded the Emirate of Granada. It took nearly two centuries to complete. Built on the hill that overlooks Granada, it was designed to be a heaven on earth."

No questions, so I went on.

"Even before entering, you know it's a special place. Your pace slows, yet your heart races. There is a trembling, a quickening. You place yourself in the minds of the great Islamic architects, and you imagine their vision."

The room became quiet.

"To walk the *Alhambra* is to meditate. One step, then the next. Not too fast, not too slow. You must walk, and see. The white of the snow behind. The yellow of the flowers ahead. You must feel the breeze on your cheeks, and the path beneath your feet. And then, looking wide, you will see one slice of the monument itself, and a vista. After a while, you slowly begin to focus. On the entrances and the exits. The stairs, up and down. Where stone meets wood. And light meets shadow."

A hand goes up. It's Grace.

"But Papa, tell us about the Nasrid Palaces."

"You will think that you're prepared, Grace, but you won't be. Nothing can really prepare you for what awaits."

"Like what," asked Oliver. "I want to know what it's like inside."

Travels with Pa

I told him that words are inadequate, that only pictures would suffice. So I asked Liam to get my iPad as the others drew closer. Page after slowly turned page came and went, as we walked through that heaven on earth.

"But what about the ceilings?" asked Charlotte. "You know I like to look up."

And we found them.

"And water," said Lorelei. "Can we swim there?"

"There are pools," I told her. "But I don't think they allow swimming."

"Are there designs, Papa?" asked Nora. "You know how much I like to draw."

And we found them too.

On and on we went, right through dinner. Finally, Freddie spoke up.

"Papa, I like the *Alhambra* a lot, but won't I be really tired?"

"Of course you will, Freddie. And your feet will be sore. But if you walk just a little while longer, you will come upon an orange grove, where you can lay in the cool. And while you rest, you can pick an orange and taste it, and you'll find that it's good. And after you've rested, you'll begin the walk back down to Granada, recalling all that you saw at the *Alhambra*. And you will wonder,

"What is Heaven anyway?"

Book Ends

January 25

We were up early and rested. Our stay at the *Palacio De Los Navas*, though brief, was pleasant and a notch above the norm. The bed, one of the best. And the breakfast all we could hope for. We particularly enjoyed our conversations with Andrés at the front desk. Competent and well mannered, he could have played the role of *receptionist de hotel* in an old Gregory Peck movie. I considered asking Andrés for a photo, but thought the better of it. A discrete man, I didn't want to offend.

The train from Granada to Barcelona was on a bullet, likely one of the originals, as there were no outlets for charging. Nevertheless, it was a whisper quiet ride with speeds up to 300 kmh. Six hours from station to station, it was a melancholy ride, as long train rides often are. Traveling northeast toward Cordoba, then north, we left the *Sierra Nevadas* behind long before sunrise. As the landscape opened one could imagine Don Quixote astride Rocinante off in the distance, Sancho Panza at their side.

Hours passed and sunshine gave way to cloudy skies. After a while, Pa asked if he might see my photos.

"Those are nice my boy. But there are no power lines or warehouses or the other modern things we've passed."

I told him I prefer to see things as I'd like them to be, not as they are.

He chuckled,

"Now you sound like old Don Quixote,"

Travels with Pa

and he commenced to quote M. Cervantes verbatim:

"Look there, Sancho Panza, my friend, and see those thirty or so wild giants, with whom I intend to do battle and kill each and all of them, so with their stolen booty we can begin to enrich ourselves. This is noble, righteous warfare, for it is wonderfully useful to God to have such an evil race wiped from the face of the earth."

"What giants?" asked Sancho Panza.

"The ones you can see over there, with the huge arms, some of which are very nearly two leagues long."

"Now look, your grace," said Sancho, *"what you see over there aren't giants, but windmills, and what seems to be arms are just their sails, that go around in the wind and turn the millstone."*

"Obviously," replied Don Quixote, *"you don't know much about adventures."*

Making his point, Pa asked if he might share a few photographs of his own.

"They're the only ones I have left," he said. "I somehow misplaced the ones of Bea and the girls. This one, I was captain of our high school baseball team. And here, I was a judge. And this last one," showing me a photo with friends and colleagues at his retirement party, "that's when I was still respected."

Pa then leaned against me, as I leaned against him nearly sixty years ago. Holding each photo with reverence, I recalled snippets from an old Paul Simon song:

Can you imagine us

Years from today

Sharing a park bench quietly?

How terribly strange

To be seventy ...

And what a time it was

It was ...

A time of innocence

A time of confidences,

Long ago, it must be,

I have a photograph,

Preserve your memories

They're all that's left you.

Note To Grandchildren

January 26

Hi Kids. I visited a museum today here in Barcelona - the Museu Picasso. It's named after Pablo Picasso, a famous man born in Spain a long time ago. Mr. Picasso was an artist who expressed himself in many ways, but he especially loved to paint. The *Museu Picasso* has several of his paintings, although not all of them.

Travels with Pa

Museums all over the world display his art. You can even see one or two at the museum in Des Moines.

Pablo was a boy when he first started putting paint on paper. This is a house he painted when he was ten. And a painting of his dog at about the same time. His parents encouraged him, so he studied to become better. He was twelve when he painted this one. And a teenager when he painted these. Pablo learned a lot from his father, and other teachers, but when he left home, he started painting the world the way he saw it.

Pablo wasn't afraid to express himself in ways unique to him. There were no barriers between his imagination and the world around. Pablo liked animals a lot, but he especially liked pigeons. His father liked pigeons too, and painted this one. Pablo admired his father a lot, but saw the world differently.

So if you love pigeons, you can paint them as much as you like and for as long as you like.

There was another famous man from Spain. His name was Antonio Gaudi. He loved to draw, so much so that he became a great architect and designed many buildings. The most famous of all is here in Barcelona. Mr. Gaudi once said something I think is very important:

To do things right, first you need love, then technique.

So whatever you choose to do with your life, love it first then get very good at it.

Love, Papa

P.S. If it's painting you come to love, the world will be your canvas.

And You Look Up

January 27

Just outside my window is a small church, Sant Jaume. Not far is another church, *de la Basílica de la Sagrada Família*. Visitors come from all of the world to wonder. An architect friend told me I shouldn't miss it, and that I should prepare. So I learned that in the mid-19th century Barcelona was modernized, resulting in a significant expansion of its city limits. Talk began about the construction of a grand cathedral. On December 31, 1881, a group calling itself the Spiritual Association of Devotees of St. Joseph acquired a large plot of land upon which to build. Architect Francisco del Villar was commissioned to head up the project. Resigning after just a year, del Villar was succeeded by Antoni Gaudi i Cornet. Barely thirty years old, Gaudi devoted the remaining 43 years of his life to the project.

While Gaudi was alive, construction began on the crypt, apse façade, first sections of the cloister and the Nativity façade. Fearing there would be times during which resources would be scarce, Gaudi planned the construction in phases. He believed this would make it more difficult for the project to be abandoned.

Gaudi experimented with scale plaster models which he thought were more effective than plans. The models and drawings left behind after his death in 1926 made it possible for subsequent architects to remain true to his work. The *Sagrada Família Basilica*, still unfinished, is now a UNESCO world heritage site.

With that bit of history, and a pleasant walk through old Barcelona, you arrive - your pace slows; you imagine the mind of Gaudi. Entering, you are welcomed, the organ announces the hour, and the soprano begins:

Ave Maria Gratia plena Maria, gratia plena Maria, gratia plena ...

And you look up, see all around, keep looking, and seeing, and time ceases. The hour is announced again and you're reminded of that old, dead language:

Pater Noster qui es in caelis,

sanctificetur nomen tuum.

Adveniat regnum tuum.

Fiat voluntas tua,

sicut in caelo et in terra ...

And in some inexplicable way, it comes to life.

Our Father,

Who art in heaven,

hallowed be Thy name.

Thy kingdom come.

Thy will be done on earth,

as it is in heaven ...

Again you wonder, finally leave, look up one last time, and remember Gaudi's words:

Glory is light, light gives joy, and joy is the happiness of the spirit.

And, in the moment, the reality of the world in which we live makes little difference.

The Guest House

January 28

Juliann and Adam visited Barcelona a few years ago, before Lorelai was born. It's difficult these days to keep track of such things, birthdates of grandkids included. Even when the kids were younger I'd struggle to get their names right, especially the girls. It might take two or three attempts, four on occasion. They didn't seem to mind, and rarely corrected me. Perhaps they thought they might escape some consequence if I misidentified them. Anyway, Ju and Adam had a wonderful time in this high energy city, reminding me a few days ago of its highlights.

For Adam, an evening at the Ziryab Shisha Lounge is a must. He couldn't recall the location but knew the neighborhood. The Ziryab, I discovered, was just a ten minute walk from the Hostal Fernando, tucked away quietly in a maze of side streets and alleys where the best places are often found. Arriving shortly after 6:00, I was greeted with a sign by a pleasant young man. You see, everyone employed at the Ziryab is hearing impaired. Their silence is calming. With a menu in hand, he led me up narrow stairs, offering one of two rooms. I chose the one on the right, just because. Settling in, I studied the menu.

Travels with Pa

Having visited Istanbul several years ago, I know a little about *shisha*, or hookah tobacco, a mixture of dried herbs or fruits, tobacco, glycerin, and molasses. I ordered the *Al Fakher* (the Classic Middle Eastern) with a passion fruit mix. While waiting, I sipped on a black tea with cardamom and visited with two young men who'd settled in before me.

One left Croatia for Barcelona five years ago for work, fell in love, and stayed. The other, a native with roots going back generations. They meet at the Ziryab once a month, without fail, for shisha and good company.

A young woman arrived, set up my hookah bowl with pipe, and gently placed three hot coals evenly spaced around the rim. Throughout the evening she replenished the coals a half dozen times. An ample *shisha* mix, as mine was, will last up to three hours.

An hour in, three young women arrived shortly after the young men left. Yael, born and raised in Kenya by Jewish-Bolivian parents, is an accomplished artist committed to wildlife preservation. Lourdes, an educator and community activist, will return to El Salvador someday (after her travel is completed) to help rebuild communities. And Lorna, from Dublin with a master's degree in international law, will soon begin work with an NGO in Guatemala. Three women informed, passionate, and committed to making things better.

For two hours the talk ranged from human rights to privilege, oppression and wealth distribution, to making one's way in a world without roadmaps. It was a wonderful evening. Only one thing would have made it better, to have had my daughters pres-

Travels with Pa

ent, sharing in the conversation, and the *shisha*. The women had yoga in the morning - on the pier - and so left before Pa and me.

Alone with my hookah, I fixed my attention on a favorite poem, framed on a wall nearby:

This being human is a guest house.

Every morning a new arrival.

A joy, a depression, a meanness, some momentary awareness comes

as an unexpected visitor.

Welcome and entertain them all! Even if they are a crowd of sorrows, who violently sweep your house empty of its furniture,

still, treat each guest honorably. He may be clearing you out

for some new delight. The dark thought, the shame, the malice. meet them at the door laughing and

invite them in. Be grateful for whatever comes. because each has been sent as a guide from beyond.

    -Rumi

CHAPTER THREE
Italy

So We Get Off The Ferry

January 29

The voyage from Barcelona to Genoa was pleasant and uneventful. Old but serviceable, the 9 level "MN/Excellent" cut through the rough seas with ease, delivering us an hour ahead of schedule. Pa and I disembarked quickly and within minutes were in the queue for passport control, ahead of us just a gentleman and his dog. That's when the adventure began.

Turns out, either the man or his dog, or both, weren't liked. 30 minutes passed before we were checked through. They didn't bother to inquire of Pa's credentials. Shortly after, we were in the duty store on the lookout for a taxi. A sign directed us to the street, but there were no taxis, ever. Another 30 minutes passed and we headed out on foot, placing limited faith in the offline navigator app. Right off, it was confused. Fortunately, I'd taken a screen shot of the route, and so knew the general direction. But knowing west to east only gets you so far.

Good fortune struck, however. A taxi driver stopped to inquire if we needed help. Opening up Notes, I showed him the Palazzo Zecchino spelled out and the address in Italian. He assured us he would get us there. 20 minutes passed. I wanted to believe we were closer, but really had no way of knowing. The kind man finally admitted that he didn't either. He did promise to get us as far as the Piazza Caricamento, beyond which only pedestrians are allowed. Beggars can't be choosers so we stayed with him another 10 minutes, then exited. With a warm Genoese smile, he wished us well.

The adventure continued. One kind person after another offered to help. The last, a kindly old man just closing his book shop for the day, walked us as far as the Basilica del Vigne. Taking my hand, he offered assurance that the Palazzo Zecchino was just on the other side. A good 15 minutes passed and we were back at the Basilica. Trusting T-Mobile to put a call through, we made contact with Leonardo. He assured us we were close, but to stay put. 15 minutes later his young associate arrived. Another 10 minutes and we there.

The Palazzo Zecchino is ancient, possibly as old as the Colosseum. Built to withstand the centuries, no wood was used in its construction. After Leonardo's associate instructed us as to the use of each of the four keys we were given, she escorted us up eight flights to 10A. Utilizing the last two of the keys, we were in. A lovely room, but very cold. The associate having departed, we located the steam radiator and turned the knob counterclockwise. A gurgling noise suggested it was alive. But 5PM came and went and I was still in my down jacket. I called Leonardo. He promised to come over. And he did, on his black Vespa with matching black helmet and jacket. After sometime Leonardo diagnosed the problem and made the repair. He assured us it was working but that we probably wouldn't notice an improvement for at least an hour.

"You might want to go out."

The sun long set, it was very dark. The dilemma, risk frostbite, or risk getting lost, never to be found again. We chose the latter, determined to take the advice of a good friend:

"If you're unsure, or even unsure if you're unsure, take photos of landmarks."

We set out again. One little street, then another, propositioned at one point by a woman who called me handsome. She took it back when I said, "no thanks." We finally made our way onto a fairly well lighted street, taking a peek into a most amazing space, the Oratory of Saint Fillipo Neri. The lights on and door unlocked, we entered. It had the look and feel of a miniature Sistine Chapel. A little man came out, introduced himself as Giorgio Giovanni, and for the next while, he proudly recited a history lesson in great detail.

Finally, we asked if he might know of a good restaurant nearby. "Certo," he said and proceeded to walk us across the street to his friend's place. Perusing the menu, I ordered and was soon served what seemed to be a very authentic plate of ravioli.

Well satisfied and confident in our landmarks, we made it back to our warm room and comfortable bed.

Just A Few Things

January 30

Some readers have been wondering about Pa. In particular, why is it he's not around at times. An example, the evening at the

Travels with Pa

Ziryab Shisha Lounge where he never made an appearance.

You see, Pa was very health conscious. Still is. As an athlete, he was forbidden to smoke or drink. That stuck with him. In college he did some research and made up his own mind. Tobacco and alcohol wouldn't serve him well in the long run. The same with sugar. Pa was fortunate to not have a sweet tooth. That also served him well. If Pa had a vice, it was ice cream. He could justify ice cream. It had milk, and milk is good for your body. Besides, over his long life he never saw that ice cream caused anyone any harm.

We've stopped for ice cream a couple of times. Pa encourages it.

"If it had been bad for me, I wouldn't have lived to be ninety-five," he stated with some authority.

"Good point," I responded, not in the mood to instruct him on rudimentary genetics.

Pa being Dutch might have something to do with it. The Dutch have long been a fastidious people. Their tendency toward high standards perhaps a contributing factor.

By the way, we're in Florence, having arrived late yesterday. We booked three nights at the Villa Merlo Bianco, a convent run by the Suore di San Giovanni Battista (Sisters of St. John the Baptist). We've yet to look around, but it appears to be quite a place.

According to the literature, the Villa was built sometime in the fifth century, then rebuilt in 1529 after the Spanish siege of Florence. For centuries it was an estate for wealthy barons, falling into disrepair early in the 20th century. During World War II, the Allies used it as a command post. At the war's conclusion, the good sisters took it over, restoring it as a safe haven for travelers.

The Villa offers breakfast but no other meals, so Pa and I hit the streets in search of something authentic. We happened upon the Vecchia Osteria del Nacchero in a quiet neighborhood nearby. A small place, it looked authentic, with service beginning at 7:00. As it was 6:55, and the door slightly ajar, we stepped in. On the far side of the room, around a large table, was a "family" finishing its meal. This wasn't a family with little kids, just adults, two generations at least. The patriarch, in a tone that chilled me to the bone, barked "Five minutes!" I felt like the young man who'd been dating his daughter and he'd just found out about it. Then it crossed my mind that this might be some kind of "planning meeting", the subject of which was a secret not to be shared beyond the table.

Whatever the reason for the greeting, Pa and I backed out slowly. A block away, we found a Chinese place where we were welcomed warmly and treated like family.

A Good Day To Be Sick

January 31

I've got a cold. I'm not complaining, but it has slowed me down a bit. Fortunately, it hasn't affected Pa, immune as he is to everything.

"Not quite everything," he corrected me. "I've not been out of my body long enough to have complete immunity."

Travels with Pa

Anyway, I talked with Sarah, my daughter the physician, who advised that I take a day off. So I did, and it was a good day. But first things first. I need to get something off my chest. "Confession is good for the soul," or so I was taught as a boy.

As those who have traveled much are well aware, a certain moral decline can occur. Nothing significant at first, but one thing can lead to another. It started small, as it almost always does. Filching a sugar packet or two, like the forbidden cookie taken from grandmother's jar. Then the extra napkins, and the tea bags. Of course they'd never be missed. But it all adds up.

But why now? I suppose being at the convent has got me to this point. The nun singing sweetly this morning in the room just beyond the dining area. Or the crucifix above my bed. I do take some consolation from the thief on the cross who asked forgiveness and it was granted. Nevertheless, it seems there must be some atonement.

So I've made a promise (rather than a vow which carries greater consequences when broken) to make an annual Christmas gift to the Sisters of St. John the Baptist. It's on my Calendar as a recurring event, and in my Contacts for easy access. I've yet to decide whether the annual gift covers future pilfering. Perhaps some monk in Nepal will offer guidance.

Back to my good day. I got my laundry done! Having asked Sister Jo (Jocelyn) where I might find a *lavanderia a gettoni*, she gestured to take a right, and proceed until I got to the Coop. Trusting her in all ways, I eventually saw it off in the distance, made my way there, then started the search.

After some time I was questioned about my needs.

"Ho bisogna di una lavanderia a gettoni,"

I responded with Google translate. The kind lady walked me to the far side of the store, depositing me at the Lavanderie. To my chagrin, however, I learned that it wasn't self-serve and I'd have to leave all that I owned but the clothes on my back. Not willing to take the chance, I walked outside and asked Siri for directions to the nearest laundromat. Within minutes I was there, and confused.

I eventually surmised that there is a central mainframe that controls everything. The machine you use, the soap, the length of time, the euros. But then what? Fortunately, a grandmotherly type, they're the best, interceded. Taking my clothes, and my money, she made it all happen. And now my clothes are clean for the first time in a month.

Feeling on top of the world, we walked across the street to a little bookstore where the nicest woman directed me to the lone shelf with English titles. Selecting Robert Harris' *Pompeii* (seemed appropriate) I gladly paid the 12 Euros and was on my way.

Wandering about, and not caring if we were lost or not, we eventually made our way home. And there we sat, in the warmth of the afternoon, enjoying the view.

Spirit Concealed In Matter

February 1

We thought we were up early. But making our way to the dining room, it was apparent that the good sisters start their day well before we do. Bustling about, each was engaged in some task with great attention but without fanfare. Not a one of them over five feet, they dressed in black but for a splash of white around their faces. I've always appreciated the nuns, having been "raised" by them through the eighth grade. Most likely they have their squabbles, but to a young boy they always appeared to put the other before self.

Pa and I were out the door by mid-morning. Our destination, the Florence of museums, churches, history, and photographs. But as often occurs, there are discoveries along the way.

The dogs and their companions. The joggers and bicyclists. The Old Friends, and the young ones. Nonno e Nona. The second story man, and the flower people. The tiny cars, and the bridges. The tour groups and the risk taker. The side streets and the hidden places. One, in particular, intrigued us. The workshop of a chemist or, perhaps, an alchemist. A white coated gentleman welcomed us, then continued his work. Looking about quietly, I finally summoned the courage to inquire if he was an alchemist.

"Si, naturalmente." I asked if he knew of Carl Jung, the Swiss psychiatrist. The name didn't register.

I elaborated, "He wrote extensively about the psychology of alchemy." "Si si!"

I then located a quote of Jung's:

When the alchemist speaks of Mercurius, on the face of it he means quicksilver (mercury), but inwardly he means the world-creating spirit concealed or imprisoned in matter.

Travels with Pa

Quando l'alchimista parla di Mercurio, a prima vista intende l'argento vivo (mercurio), ma interiormente intende lo spirito creatore del mondo nascosto o imprigionato nella materia.

He studied it carefully, then responded with a big smile, *bene molto bene!* and returned to his work.

We stayed a few minutes longer before exiting onto the street which opened onto a large plaza and the Basilica di Santa Maria Novella.

We considered John's Gospel: *"And the world became flesh…"* and wondered why it was that the Church never tolerated alchemists. And then the Gospel of Thomas (suppressed by the early Church Fathers) came to mind:

Split a piece of wood: I am there. Lift a stone, and you will find me there.

So Zen like.

After lingering, we began the walk back, enjoying the warm afternoon and pondering questions interesting and provocative.

How is it that birds know which rock to sit on, or with whom to mate? And to where might Jesus have traveled after leaving home and before going public.

Tomorrow, the Uffizi.

Travels with Pa

Always A Tourist

February 2

Our last morning in Florence. The Uffizi then the train to Salerno.

We wandered, as usual, arriving at the Uffizi just in time for our assigned entry. Second visit for me, first for Pa. Same rules as before, we'd devote most of our attention to what attracted him. Fair enough. I can return someday. It's likely he won't have the opportunity. Needing a host, it might be difficult for someone else to tolerate Pa's idiosyncrasies as I do. That's not to say I don't enjoy Pa's company, but the elderly tend to be set in their ways. I'm sure others will say the same about me soon enough. They may already.

Back to the Uffizi. Incredible! Not enough time, or stamina. I won't bother the reader with endless photos. Nothing compares with being there. An online visit a close second: https://www.uffizi.it/en/the-uffizi

I do want to share, however, what was of particular interest to Pa. No surprise. Though we reminisce about the days of our youth, often with a sense of loss, we most identify with those like us. I, on the other hand, am not quite there yet, or so I say.

My preference is the narratives, those that tell a story. And those, though few, that celebrate the strength of women. Of course the classics will forever be classic. And timeless as well, renderings of those who challenged the powerful and lost. Then there was the guy, so much the young Italian male posing for his girlfriend.

Back on the street, we were reminded once again that, when in Florence, one is always a tourist.

Had We Not Stopped…

February 3

Pa wanted to visit Sicily. The parents of a boyhood friend had immigrated from there. He loved listening to their Italian, and eating the mounds of pasta his friend's mother served, topped with sausage and sauce. On the map, it's a straight shot from Florence to Messina. On the train app it looked relatively easy as well, just a single transfer in Salerno. Rather than make a very long day of it, we decided to spend the night there. A throwback to the '50s, Salerno isn't a major tourist stop.

But had we not stopped, we would not have walked its streets, or its seaside esplanade, or met Angela, proprietress of the Holiday Guesthouse who taught us all we needed to know about Italian mothers and their sons.

Had we not stopped, we would not have found the little place serving *pane e prosciutto*, and had a sunny picnic lunch while waiting for the train.

But had we stayed in Salerno, we would not have enjoyed the train ride south along the Amalfi coast, arrived in Messina by high-speed ferry, ate in our first Sicilian restaurant, and feasted on our first Sicilian pizza.

Had we stayed in Salerno, we would not have had a room with

such a view.

Palermo

February 4

We didn't know what to expect of Palermo, its name familiar, but little else. Some fly into the Falcone Borsellino Airport, rent a car, then drive south for the beaches and the ruins, never setting foot in Sicily's administrative capital. Some stop to visit the Cattedrale di Palermo and little else. Others winter annually in this city by the sea, like the two gentlemen we met at dinner last night. In their 80s, one from London and the other Munich, they've visited every January since retirement, staying till spring and the blooming of crocuses back home. Still others come for a winter holiday and never leave. For example, the couple dining to our right. Pittsburgh Steeler fans most of their lives, they promised to relocate to a land without ice and snow once the kids left and were settled. That's been a decade now. These days, they get back every April and October, beating the peak season fares. The children visit when they can.

What Pa and I discovered when we arrived, is that Palermo is an old city, with little to suggest the glitz of other Italian metropolises to the north. It has a different feel as well. Understandably so, as Palermo is closer to northern Africa than Rome. There's been no urban renewal here, and we like that. Walk the Via Roma from the *Stazione* to our Hostal and there's much to see, and discover as well if you take the time to look down, and stay long enough to enjoy pig intestines at their best.

But Palermo experiences a metamorphosis with the departure of daylight. There's a different feel, as the lights of night have an irresistible attraction.

Village On A Hill

February 5

We wanted to get out into the countryside. As wonderful as Palermo is, and Florence, Barcelona, and Lisbon, there comes a time when the senses need a break. There's only so much that can be processed. It seems that if one remains too long on the streets and in the museums, you become numb to all of it. I suppose that happens to all of us, no matter where we live. A wonderful thing about traveling is the ease with which the scenery can be changed. Today the churches and markets. This evening a quaint restaurant. Tomorrow the mountains.

With a map of Sicily spread before us, and Google within easy reach, we chose Gangi, a hilltop town just a couple of hours from Palermo. Having determined our destination, we rented a car from Hertz and reserved a room with Booking.com. It was that simple. Wanting to spend most of the day in Palermo, we arranged to pick the car up at 4, early enough to arrive at the B&B IL Galletto by sunset. It was a good plan.

The first hour or so was easy, and the scenery stunning. But the A19 could only get us so close. Inevitably, we would have to take the off ramp and hope the GPS wouldn't fail us. And it didn't, for the most part. But daylight did. And with its diminishment came uncertainty. Twists and turns easy to maneuver at high noon become challenges that have to be mastered. And, as time went on, signs of human habitation diminished, giving way to other creatures.

Sunset gave way to night, but somehow, like the proverbial golden city on the mountain top, Gangi appeared and we were nearly home. Of course rarely are things that easy. Once we arrived in the town center, our navigational aid hiccupped and we were left to our own devices in a thousand-year-old town that never anticipated the arrival of automobiles.

We don't know how long it took to work our way out of that maze in which there was barely an inch on either side of our Jeep. And turning around was beyond all possibility. But somehow we got to the other end, arriving two hours later than expected.

I asked Pa how he thought we were able to make it. "Dutch perseverance," he insisted. I gave full credit to the St. Christopher medal tucked deep in my wallet. If there's ever been a land where such a talisman was needed, it's Sicily.

Fabio

February 6

I'd be remiss if I didn't share an incident, from our stay in Gangi.

It was Sunday and breakfast was meager. Sweet bread, a liquidly yogurt, and an orange from the previous season. I would have

Travels with Pa

liked to have had coffee but couldn't figure out the machine. Shortly after, Pa and I went for a walk, returning to our room as cold as it was during the night. Giorgio and Nina apparently as frugal as the nuns in Florence. With a wind from the west howling relentlessly, there was nothing to do but crawl under the great mound of blankets and read.

2PM arrived and I was famished. I hate using that word as it speaks of privilege. Let's just say I was very hungry. But it was Sunday, and nothing is open in Gangi on Sunday. Managing to back the Jeep down the street, we went searching. On the outskirts, apparently out of reach of the parish priest, was the Miramonti, a simple place as inviting as you'll find. Mid-afternoon and the coffee klatch was there, and the fellows who, any other day, would be at the local bar.

A very nice woman, Protestant looking, handed me a menu. I scanned it quickly and inquired about the lasagna. With a wink and a smile she took our order, returning soon with the finest lasagna I'd ever laid eyes on. Pa as well. Rest assured, there's none finer in Iowa. I ordered seconds along with a salad, bread with olive oil, and a Coca-Cola, second to wine as the favorite drink of Sicilians.

The wind still howling, we considered waiting until morning to fill the tank. But the Miramonti isn't open on Monday and neither are its gas pumps. So we pulled up next to one of the relics, removed the cap, and found quite a surprise. Not knowing how to handle it, I took a photo and went inside for assistance. My waitress immediately called for Fabio, a little guy with obvious street smarts, and directed him to help. We were off.

Travels with Pa

And here's where my utter stupidity is revealed. I assumed Fabio knew a better filling station down the road. But within minutes we'd pulled up to one of a different kind and exited. Fabio then directed that I pop the trunk where he grabbed the needed apparatus. Problem was, I don't believe he'd ever used one. Try as he might, he never got it to work, and was shaking like a leaf from the arctic blast. Not wanting to impose any longer, I took him back to the Miramonti and handed him a twenty. You'd have thought he'd won the *SuperEnalotto*.

Back in front of our place we sat, staring at the Jeep's control panel, and wondering if we might make it to Agrigento the next day and the Hertz office. And then the revelation - "Hybrid" in big orange letters. *Mama mia!* Braving the wind, we circumnavigated the Jeep, finding a second fuel door on the opposite side. Of course!

So back to the Miramonti we went, pulling up on Pa's side, and confident of the outcome. But we couldn't get the VISA card to work, or the Euro feeder. So back inside, Fabio just where he was when we first made his acquaintance.

Now here's where it gets a little murky. Fabio couldn't get the VISA to work either so he asked for a twenty. He then directed that I handle the pump while he fed the machine. Soon enough, some number of liters were deposited. With a big slap on the back for Fabio, Pa and I were on our way again.

That evening I checked my CapitalOne balance. Dining at the Miramonti – $18.05. Gas at the Miramonti – $21.88 ($20 + the exchange fee).

Gotta hand it to Fabio. He's got street smarts.

Travels with Pa

The Open Road

February 7–8

We left early, having packed an orange, apple and croissant for the road. Coffee would have to wait. Our general intent was to wander for two days, returning the car in Messina the end of the second. From there we'd cross the Strait of Messina by ferry, arriving in San Giovanni at nightfall.

We did have two planned stops, UNESCO sites of significant importance. Google maps predicted a two-hour drive to the Villa Romana del Casale.

Arriving in four, the effort was worth it. The Villa, 3km south of Piazza Armerina, had been a large Roman palace. Two plausible theories are suggested as to its original ownership. One, that it was built in the early 4th century by a Roman senator engaged in the import of wild animals. A second, that it was the country home of the Emperor Maximian. The size of the original villa - 60 rooms on four levels - suggests to historians it had an imperial owner. Excavation of the villa revealed it to be home of one of the richest collections of Roman mosaics in the world, almost 40,000 square feet of mosaic floors, well preserved due to a massive landslide in the 1300s.

Off-season and a Monday, we had the site to ourselves but for a Berlin couple. Pa, knowing some German, chose to follow them, leaving me to photograph the highly detailed figures. The Berlin couple left just as I finished, allowing us the opportunity for a solitary stroll, imagining what life was like for the privileged of Rome before the Fall of the Empire a century later.

Travels with Pa

Our next stop was the Valley of the Temples, northwest then southwest, near Agrigento and the southern coast. Founded as a Greek colony in the 6th century, Agrigento became a major municipality in the Mediterranean region.

Little exists of the original city with the exception of the sacred hill above it. But that's what brought us there. Overlooking modern Agrigento, the plain surrounding it and the Mediterranean beyond, are the remains of Doric temples and the remnants of an early Christian burial ground.

Walking at dusk, we felt ourselves in a time capsule of reverence, no matter the beliefs of the Greeks, Romans, and Christians who honored the site for reasons unique to their worldviews. After a quiet night at the Gocci di Girgenti, we were on the road in good time in the morning. Without agenda and free to roam, we appreciated the old and arrival of the new.

Last night we rested at the Villa Princi, the narrow passage connecting the Tyrrhenian Sea with the Ionian just beyond our reach. And this morning we slept in, picnicking at the foot of the town monument a block from the *Stazione*.

Both Pa and I mused that the anonymous figure, sculpted by Rocco Larussa (1825–1894) bears a very close resemblance to old Walt Whitman (1819–1892).

One has to wonder if Walt and Rocco ever met on the open road.

Afoot and light-hearted

I take to the open road,

Healthy, free, the world before me,

The long brown path before me

leading wherever I choose.

Henceforth I ask not good fortune,

I myself am good fortune,

Henceforth I whimper no more,

postpone no more, need nothing,

Done with indoor complaints,

libraries, querulous criticisms,

Strong and content I travel the open road …

Nonna Maria Aka Giuseppe

February 9

Several weeks ago we decided to take the ferry to Patras, rather than the longer journey around northern Italy to Greece. There being no easy way to get from San Giovanni to Brindisi, we chose to spend a couple of days along the way in Taranto.

The leg to Paola went as scheduled, as did Paola to Sibari, where we'd have a short wait. Arriving in the rain, we discovered the wait would be longer, due to a sixty-minute train delay. It being an open-air station and the temperature hovering around forty,

Travels with Pa

we headed out, finding a little kabob place nearby. What looked good on the menu was wanting in some respects. Nevertheless, it was filling.

Returning to the station, the 564 eventually arrived with an engineer intent on making up for lost time. Somehow he shaved thirty minutes off the projected two hours, pulling into his final stop with the Italians on board generally pleased with the outcome. But it was dark, with no apparent way to get the 3 miles to Nonna Maria's B&B but to walk.

It's a funny thing about Italian taxi drivers. They seem to know when someone is on foot. Within a block we had a ride. Ten minutes later we were there. Or so we thought. Up and down the street we looked for Nonna's place, but without success.

Finally we asked a tall lanky fellow lurking in the shadows. Of course he knew the place, and within a couple of minutes we were buzzing for Nonna. A young man showed up at the door, introducing himself as Giuseppe. Nonna's son we assumed.

Turns out there is no Nonna. Being an entrepreneur, Giuseppe owns four B&Bs and is in the process of buying a hotel, he thought foreigners would be more likely to book at Nonna's rather than Giuseppe's. Fair enough. But then we were told we wouldn't be staying there as he had a "very nice place" for us just down the street. We got a little suspicious, but what were the options? Five minutes later and on a deserted side street, we were there. It went well after that, and soon we were curled up with Harris' *Pompeii*, two days before the eruption with nearly everyone clueless.

By ten it was lights out, but then midnight and an incoming text from Juliann. She'd sent a new tune by The Lone Bellow –

Homesick.

If you're homesick

It's your heart telling your mind that you love somebody

If you got regrets

There's a possibility that you got something to check off your list

It's a long walk home and a short life to live…

Hmmmmm. I think Ju meant well, but it kept us up for a while, thinking about loneliness, and solitude, and the considerable differences. The ache of one and the necessity of the other.

After a while I went to Notes, where I keep and regularly add to a number of Folders – Recipes, Good Reads, Inspiration, Poems, Quotes. I started browsing, looking for reminders.

There was Nietzsche.

No one can build you the bridge on which you, and only you, must cross the river of life.

Hermann Hesse:

You must unlearn the habit of being someone else or nothing at all, of imitating the voices of others and mistaking the faces of others for your own.

E.E. Cummings:

To be but yourself, in a world which is doing its best, night and day,

Travels with Pa

to make you everybody else, means to fight the hardest battle which one human being could fight.

And the short-story writer Elizabeth Bishop:

…I now see a wonderful cold rocky shore in the Falklands, or a house in Nova Scotia on the bay, exactly like my grandmother's, unbearable as the reality would be.

But I think everyone should go through a stretch of it. Perhaps it's a recurrent need.

About the time Ju was eighteen, I gave her a copy of a poem by Mary Oliver, *The Journey*. A month ago she sent it back to me with a thank you, having found inspiration at a time when she was considering a major career change that would require her, Adam, Lorelai and Freddie to relocate.

…but little by little,

as you left their voices behind,

the stars began to burn

through the sheets of clouds,

and there was a new voice,

which you slowly

recognized as your own,

that kept you company

as you strode deeper and deeper

into the world,

determined to do

the only thing you could do,

determined to save

the only life you could save.

The Difference Of A Day

February 1

We weren't too keen on Taranto that first night, for reasons previously stated. But in the morning we thought we'd better give it a chance. Considering its seaside location, and its history dating back to the ancient Spartans, it must surely be worth two days.

Heading out, I was reminded that we were staying in somewhat of a depressed area, and wondered if it might get better. Walking toward the waterfront and then along it, I had doubts.

But then Pa turned our attention to the little things, those unaffected by human conflict and independent of economic circumstances.

"Look around, young man," he said. "There is always beauty if you're open to it. Mystery too. The oddities of nature inform us."

Oh Pa, Dutch that he is, he's actually quite the optimist.

"Look at that fellow," he said, pointing to a gentleman feeding a cat. "Where would we be without the kindness of strangers?"

My whole outlook had changed in the brief time we'd been walking. Then I pointed ahead for Pa's benefit.

"Look at that. A young artist just getting started."

Our focus shifted to the creative impulse of humans in its myriad forms, and the efforts of some to attend to community needs through public improvements. We continued, arriving at the entrance of the Old Town, and an inviting little place still serving lunch. The menu wasn't exhaustive, but a delicious meal could be pieced together. Fried mussels raised locally. Steamed shrimp, caught offshore. Olives grown nearby. And bread dipped in the local oil. If that wasn't sufficient, meeting Pierre Francesco and his boss, Mattia, made our day.

We first talked about Taranto, and the many good things happening. Then travel. Mattia recently completed a motorcycle trip starting in Lisbon, then southern Portugal, southern Spain, Barcelona, finally returning home the full length of Italy. We shared stories. Pierre is about to leave for Los Angeles where he'll visit his best friend from elementary school. The two of them plan to spend a long weekend in Las Vegas. I told him it's like an adult Disney Land. He smiled, "What happens in Vegas stays in Vegas."

Mattia needed to tend to other business, but before leaving offered me a glass of the House Red, on the house. We shook hands and I told him we'd be back, having already mentioned Pa. He liked that. "Ancestors are very important to us Italians."

Alone with Pierre, we visited a while longer. I asked if he considered himself Greek or Roman, or both. He shook his head. "We're Spartans." I asked if he'd seen the movie *The 300 Spartans*. Big smile. "That's us." We talked about school. He's just about finished his studies in Maritime Trade at the local university. And we talked about family.

"Are you married? "We Spartans don't marry," he said. "At least not early. But I have a girlfriend." I asked what she thought about his position. "She's a Spartan too." Big smile again. He then showed me photos of Maria. Oh my. I told him that she's very beautiful. "Of course," he said with the biggest smile yet. "She's a Spartan."

New customers arrived, so we shook hands, promising to visit the nearby Archeological Museum and learn all about the Spartans.

Taking a different route back, we passed through a seaside park, stopping to pay homage to an Old Master. From there, down a recently revitalized stretch of shops and businesses. Turning the corner and a couple of blocks later, we were back on "Nonna's street" and then ours, still deserted, but much less menacing than the evening before.

Città Fantasma

February 11

Giuseppe stopped by to see how we were doing. A very nice surprise. We talked about his business and plans for the future. "This is a good time to be investing in Taranto," he said. "There's a new mayor in town, Renaldo Melucci." Giuseppe knows the mayor personally and proceeded to make the connection. I lost him after the third cousin. Anyway, Mayor Melucci has a fondness for history, particularly that of Taranto and the Puglia region. He believes the future of the city lies, in part, in its past. Giuseppe went on, obviously proud of Taranto's ancient roots. He reminded me of Pierre in that way.

"Do you know when we were founded?"

I replied that I thought it was a couple of thousand years ago, thinking I couldn't go wrong with such a vague dating.

"Close. The Spartans settled here in the 8th century BCE. We're Spartans. Did you know that?" I feigned ignorance, not wanting to disappoint.

Then he got a little stern. "There are two places you must visit before you leave, the Museo Archeologico Nazionale and the Città Vecchia, the Old City. It's an island. A world of its own, built on the foundation of ancient Taranto. Come back in ten years. It will have been fully restored by then."

I told him I'd heard of both (not wanting to get into an explanation about Pa) and had made plans to do so. He smiled, looked at his watch, then said *"Devo andare. Business to attend to. Just leave the key on the table on your way out."*

Pa and I visited after Giuseppe left, acknowledging that we'd mischaracterized him. So in deference to Giuseppe, and to Pierre, we promised to spend the evening in the Old City and the next morning at the Museo.

Sunset came soon enough and we were at the entrance. It's an extraordinary place. A crumbling relic. We moved slowly as the light faded. A labyrinth of ancient streets and abandoned homes, we could feel the presence of those who'd gone before. If ever there was a ghost town, this was it.

After a while, we happened on the Cattedrale Di San Cataldo, and learned that the Byzantines built it in the 10th century. The door was open and we wandered about. More ghosts for sure.

It was getting late, so we left, wanting to get back without difficulty. Not an easy task it turned out. But then we saw the sea, and the way home.

A Funny Thing Happened…

February 12

As promised, we set aside the morning for a visit to the Museo Archeologico Nazionale. It would be an easy walk, twenty minutes on a sunny day. Out the door, one left, then another. And there we were, greeted to an unexpected sight. It appeared most of Taranto had congregated in a single locale. But of course, it was Saturday at the Market!

I had a flashback to the 60's movie, *A Funny Thing Happened on the Way to the Forum*. It was kind of like that. The day before we'd gone looking for a grocery. Just a few basics, oranges, apples, sardines, bread, perhaps some chocolate. And we were nearly out of coffee. We found a couple of storefronts, but they were lacking. Now we knew why. It was a cornucopia. A marvel of fruits and vegetables, eggs and cheeses. An abundance of mussels, and more. The feast spilled out onto nearby streets. More fruits and meats, fresh fish, clothing too. We could have lingered most of the day, but having promised Pierre and Giuseppe, couldn't go back on our word.

Moving on, we arrived at the Museo, anticipating our journey back through time. And quite a journey it was, beginning with indigenous remnants circa 6000 BCE.

Later on the ancient Greeks arrived, bringing with them their genius for beauty, and gift for community building, within which the arts and sciences, theater and music, could thrive.

Near the end of our journey, we met a young man, Domenico. Four exams away from earning his law degree, he works part-time at the Museo. He needs the money. More importantly, he has a deep reverence for the ancients and wants to absorb as much as he can before life takes over. In a most unassuming way, he shared with us his notion of the Greek ideal.

"For the Greeks, the man will die, but the ideal of the man will not. Picasso died, but the essence of Picasso lives on. So it is with the sculptor, dancer, athlete, the charioteer, even the lawyer, if he's lived a life of principle."

I asked Domenico if that's what he hopes for his life.

"It is what I want for myself. In these times it will be difficult for sure, but I believe my ancestors will guide me."

We would have liked to have learned more, but couldn't tarry as our train would leave within the hour. Wishing Domenico the best, we shook hands and departed. Walking to the *Stazione*, Pa was unusually quiet. I asked if he was troubled by something.

Travels with Pa

"I've been thinking of the young man, wondering if I lived up to the Greek ideal, for myself and those I tried to help."

I assured him he had, certainly in my eyes.

Along the way we observed others, and wondered what it is that they want for themselves and those they care about.

CHAPTER FOUR
Greece

Captain's Log

February 13

Captain's Log, Star date 2023.02.12.9:55.

Our second day aboard the MV *Grimaldi*.

The City of Brindisi, a bit rough around the edges, though still holding a measure of old-world charm. With its deep harbor, it welcomes vessels from many lands. Strange, the custom of its inhabitants to vanish in the afternoon. Mr. Spack informed me it's a daily occurrence. From 2:00 until 5:00, nearly all businesses shutter. I do wish he'd mentioned it earlier. Had he done so, I would have taken lunch aboard the *Grimaldi* and come to shore a bit later. But I hold no ill will toward the dear man. Often, we learn these things only upon disembarking. Thankfully, we had our devices.

Wandering about in the afternoon chill, I inquired:

"Scorpius, please provide directions to the nearest open restaurant."

Scorpius never ceases to amaze, its speed and precision rival that of Mr. Spack.

Within minutes we arrived at Ristorante di Giublio. After a long ascent up a single flight, had Scotty arrived before us, he surely would have beamed us, we were greeted by Mr. Giublio himself. A most affable gentleman, he seated us in a quiet corner, just across from a family with one, shall I say, very exuberant child.

Unfamiliar with the menu, we sought Mr. Giublio's recommendation.

"Ovviamente. La mia preferenza è Grandma's Orecchiette."

It was, how should I say, *fantastica*. Only later did Mr. Giublio reveal that the recipe was a closely guarded family secret, passed down from his own grandmother.

After a most leisurely meal, the wine as good as any, we prepared to leave. Bidding our goodbyes, I inquired if the evening would be busy. In so many words, he said that while Saturday nights usually are, this one would be slow.

"It's the finals of *Sanremo*, our country's national voice contest. Everyone will be in front of their televisions."

Descending the stairs, I directed Mr. Spack to update me as soon as the results were known.

Well after dark, we returned to the *Grimaldi* just as loading concluded. At 22:00 sharp, we cast off, leaving behind a city to which I hope to return, though Mr. Spack informed me that a return is unlikely. I think the world of Mr. Spack, but his lack of romantic sentiment can be off-putting at times. Nevertheless, I shall dream.

Our passage through the night and into morning was smooth. With little to occupy, I detained Mr. Spack and asked him to educate me on the land of our destination.

"It has quite a history, Captain. A noble people have resided there for untold generations. They speak a strange language, however, and use a peculiar alphabet. I suggest you familiarize yourself."

With that, he activated my monitor and directed me to the basics. I did my best for a while. But, as they say, it was all Greek to me.

Sometime later, I was roused by Mr. Spack. The man never sleeps. Pointing to the prompter's map, he informed me of our position. In five hours, we would arrive in Patras, an ancient outpost on the western frontier. Soon after, the first hints of daylight appeared.

Mr. Spack and I, as is our custom, made our rounds, confirming that all was shipshape. Gazing out to sea, I recalled the words of my great-great-great-grandfather, Ole Hansen:

"The sea is the Mother. Though a harsh disciplinarian at times, She is the lover of us all."

I never met Grandpa Ole, but he's the reason I got into this business.

The Land of Homer

February 14

Upon landing, we could feel it. Though there were trucks and cars before us, and modern buildings beyond, this was the Land of Homer, the first great storyteller, the giant of letters to whom all subsequent poets, novelists, and wanderers pay tribute.

Walking down the gangplank, I struck up a conversation with a fellow passenger. I'd seen him from a distance during transit. He appeared to be a photographer, with a particular interest in boats. I told him I'd guessed as much, and he smiled, introducing himself as Gustavo Alabiso from Germany. Handing me his card, he confirmed that yes, he is indeed a photographer.

I asked if he was on assignment.

"I'm doing work on a five-year project," he said.

"Boats?" I inquired.

"In part," he replied. "I want to make the argument, through photographs, that Africans emigrating to Europe are the cultural descendants of Ulysses."

He had me on the hook.

"They are the epic voyagers, whether on foot, by truck or van, or, of course, by boat. I believe it's important to tell their stories through that lens."

I thought I had a new friend, but he had a ferry to catch and a two-hour voyage to a distant island. I promised to email. He said he'd appreciate that.

Google Maps said it was a 5.2 km walk to the Maison Grecque, easy enough on a pleasant afternoon. But like Italian taxi drivers, perhaps more so, I was besieged by three locals, each intent on providing transport. After quite the conversation, I chose Dimitris, having talked him down from 12 euros to 8. He assured me he knew my destination and was happy with the deal. He came through, and I handed him the 8, plus 2 for the bother.

After a nap and a bit of cleaning up, we went out in search of something simple for dinner. Not much was open, but we found a little place that appeared authentic. Handed a menu I couldn't make heads or tails of, I asked the waitress for a recommendation.

"Of course," she said in very passable English, soon returning with a platter of chicken, salad, fries, and a Coca-Cola to wash it down. All for 9 euros.

On the walk back, we came upon an intriguing mural on the side of an abandoned building, a large-scale painting of Alice with the rabbit.

Grace Slick came to mind:

One pill makes you larger,

and one pill makes you small,

And the ones that mother gives you

don't do anything at all,

Go ask Alice, when she's ten feet tall...

And later:

When the men on the chessboard

get up and tell you where to go,

Travels with Pa

And you've just had some kind of mushroom

and your mind is moving slow,

Go ask Alice, I think she'll know.

The Oracle of Delphi came to mind too. No doubt Lewis Carroll is her cultural descendant.

A ways further was a small park and a memorial to those who fought in the Greek War of 1821. The Greeks, rebelling against Ottoman rule, fought for a decade before gaining independence. I thought of Pierre and the 300 Spartans, and imagined, struggle though it was, that there was little doubt the Greeks would prevail.

Having paid homage, we walked a while before returning to the Maison Grecque, where a small surprise awaited on the bedside table. Turning in, I picked up *Homer*, having long ago set him down for lack of relevance. But we're in his land now - the land of the Homeric epic, the land of Odysseus.

Sing to me, Muse, of that endlessly cunning man

who was blown off course to the ends of the earth

in the years after he plundered Troy.

He passed through the cities of many people

and learned how they thought,

and he suffered many bitter hardships upon the high seas

as he tried to save his own life

and bring his companions back to their home.

But however bravely he struggled, he could not rescue them,

fools that they were,

their own recklessness brought disaster upon them all…

Don't You Hear the Whistle Blowin'

February 15

I have seven grandchildren, each loved for who they are and how they see the world. Oliver, just turned three, loves all things that move, especially if they have engines. For the longest time, it was the machinery of construction sites. He still loves them, but lately it's boats as well. What fun he'd have here in Patras, wandering the docks, imagining life at sea. He might even make the acquaintance of old Miguel Cervantes, statue though he is, revered the world over for his imagination.

Oliver would beg him to tell stories, through the lens of his own world:

Do you see over yonder, friend Sancho, thirty or forty hulking giants? I intend to do battle with them and slay them.

When Phil was a boy, he loved baseball. But one day, I asked if we might read a book by a modern-day Cervantes. Every evening for a week, we inhabited his world. To this day, if you ask Phil, he still remembers:

Travels with Pa

He always thought of the sea as 'la mar,'

which is what people call her in Spanish when they love her.

Sometimes they said bad things of her,

but always as though she were a woman.

Some of the younger fishermen spoke of her as 'el mar,'

masculine, an opponent, even an enemy.

But the old man always thought of her as feminine,

something that gave or withheld great favors…

Oliver has added trains to his long list of beloved machines. Perhaps it's because his great-grandfather was a railroad man. On a warm day this past November, we went walking the tracks together. I can still hear him singing…

I've been working on the railroad,

All the live-long day.

I've been working on the railroad,

Just to pass the time away.

Don't you hear the whistle blowin',

Rise up so early in the morn'?

Can't you hear the captain shoutin':

"Dinah, blow your horn!"

Travels with Pa

Travel Day

February 16

I've long wanted to visit the Peloponnesus, and now have the chance. Pa, student of history that he is, shares my enthusiasm. Homer tells us it was here that Paris lured Helen, igniting the Greek world in the decade-long Trojan War. And here that Pan, the goat-legged god of shepherds and fertility, wandered the forests of Arcadia.

Intent on exploring, we soon discovered that getting around is no easy task. Train service ends in Kiato, roughly halfway between Patras and Athens. Bus service, though widely available, is difficult to figure out online. And renting a car in Patras? Impossible.

So we make a plan: go to the station, buy the necessary tickets, and the next morning take the bus and two trains to the Athens airport for a car rental. It all went well, until I broke the cardinal rule.

Arriving at the station an hour before departure, we went looking for coffee. A short walk brought us to an outdoor café serving Americanos with milk and sugar, in very large cups. It was nice to sit in the morning sun, observing university students in the company of the opposite sex. I recalled those days with fondness. Time flies in pleasant surroundings.

Pa nudges, somewhat forcefully.

"We're going to miss the bus."

Travels with Pa

I glance at my watch, grab our bag, and run, arriving just as the last passenger boards. And then...

"What if there's no toilet?"

Panic.

But halfway down the aisle, there it is, next to the steps and the exit door. One of those mini-kybos you only find abroad. Panic subsiding, we take the first window seat on the right. Ninety minutes to Kiato and our first transfer. All is well.

But twenty minutes in, the urge. Thirty minutes, necessity.

I squeeze past the rather ample woman in the seat beside us. Three steps and I'm there. But the door won't open. I know it's vacant, but retreat to my seat.

Another twenty minutes - near agony. The bus stops to let off a passenger and I approach the driver.

"Do you have a key?"

"There is one," he says. "But it's lost. Stolen, probably. Thieves will take anything."

I return defeated, and pull out my phone. Maybe a scroll through recent photos will distract me.

The Brindisi water fountain? Big mistake.

Messina? The time I accidentally turned onto the train tracks and nearly peed my pants.

The Basilica in Patras? No help. Mother Mary whispers, "Just let it be."

And Jesus? He says, "Just get off." But we're in the middle of nowhere.

Travels with Pa

I count sheep, no luck, then check my watch. We're going to be late.

But we arrive - three minutes before the train is due. We see the sign - "WC" - and make a decision. We'll miss the train and take the next. But this is Greece, and the train is late, by twenty minutes.

Taking a seat just beyond the toilet, 10 minutes pass. The urge. But the door is locked.

Somehow we make it to the airport and grab the first WC, locate the Eurocar desk, greeted by Tassos and his impeccable English.

"I see you reserved a Fiat Cabrio. Too small for you. I'm giving you a free upgrade. A very nice Toyota. Oh … it has no gas. I'm giving you a Suzuki. Not so nice, but it has gas."

I remind him that it's Valentines Day. "Did you buy your wife flowers?"

"No way. It's a commercial holiday. Legal thievery." We go over the paperwork and I sign, having already paid the 83.35. "But there's a 200 euro deposit. You'll get it back in about 21 days. Legal thievery."

We shake hands, pick up the Suzuki, and drive the two hours to Nafplio without incident. Dropping our bag off with Maria, we find a quiet place for dinner. No one's there but the owners. The wife takes my order - Fried Calamari and a Greek salad. She looks at her husband. "No calamari today, but we have sardines." Having missed lunch, we had no choice.

Taking our time, we study the old man between bites. He doesn't move for an hour. I think he could be a painting.

Back at the Polyxenia, Maria welcomes us with bedtime refreshments, a brief chat, and a good night.

Up three flights and down the hall, there's the sweetest Valentine's greeting. We let ourselves in. Tiny and a bit crooked, but very pleasant.

A Room With A View

February 17

Quite unexpectedly, we ended the day at the Pramataris in Monemvasia. It's not that we hadn't hoped to visit the tiny town on the sea. It's just that the plan had been an afternoon stop with an evening return to Nafplion. But a morning agenda, at least when traveling, should be no more than scribbles on a napkin, discarded if and when a whim arises or necessity requires it.

So we set off after a late breakfast, navigating a series of seemingly connected towns until reaching the open road. Late though it was, fog still spread across the valleys like thin silk over a beautiful body. At about noon, however, the sun took over, revealing the isolated structures doting the landscape. For a while we were tourists, pointing at this and that while cruising at 100 km/hr.

Something was amiss, though, and we knew it. Then I heard the voice of William Least Heat Moon (Blue Highways). Pa did as well:

Had I gone looking for some particular place rather than any place,

Travels with Pa

I'd never have found this spring under the sycamores ...

And the next moment there it was, a thin grove of olive trees calling for our attention. We pulled over onto a thin pad of loose rock just large enough for the Suzuki, to our left a miniature tower. Pa suggested it had a religious significance. From our vantage there was only a window. But stepping around, we discovered a door with a latch. Opening it revealed an icon of the Blessed Virgin behind a votive candle, a flame rising up.

This was a sacred place.

Our initial reaction was not to intrude. But we sat with it, arriving at the belief that it was an invitation. After paying our respects, each in our own way, we moved on.

Initially there was a defined road that led to another. But soon, just a broad path amongst the trees, and nearby a patch of grass with spring flowers making their appearance. Beyond, an old evergreen, its fruit clustered like family. We would like to have stayed, and had we a tent would have. But there was the plan to reach Monemvasia.

Making our way by Google maps we continued south, unaware that an error had been made. Admiring the stunning scenery, it was apparent we'd begun a gradual ascent. No signs for Monemvasia, but Google kept us on track. Time passed and a different sign. Surely Monemvasia was just beyond. A few minutes and we came upon the tiniest of villages. Our destination but 2.6 km beyond, we had time to linger. We would like to have stayed but the light was waning, so we continued on, following the only road possible.

After a time, the road ceased to be and a broad rocky path took its place, then it narrowed, clinging to the side of the mountain.

Why? We were but a km from our destination. It must be that we were entering through the back door.

And then Google: *"You have reached your destination."*

It turns out a pin had inadvertently been dropped in the middle of the Monemvasia wilderness.

We had to turn back. Harrowing might be an overstatement. Perhaps not.

But we made it, eventually reaching the turn for Monemvasia. Stubborn Dutch that we are, we continued on, arriving within the hour at that tiny town on the sea and the Pramataris Hotel. There, dear Ursula, rented us "a very special room, one with a view."

And What If We Hadn't Stayed?

February 18

And when we woke, we were grateful we'd stayed, if for no other reason than the sunrise. Walking the beach a block from the Pramataris, we were mesmerized by the monolith rising up from the still surface. Recalling his study of mythology, Pa suggested it might be a geologic Persephone, sinking to the underworld at night, resurrected each day by the call of the sun.

Hmmmmm … I didn't think Pa was capable of such flights of

imagination. And he surprised me again, "Let's go see what's there."

I was hesitant, reminding him that we'd planned to return to Nafplion after breakfast.

"Young man, we stayed the night. Why not stay the morning?"

There was no reason to argue. Pa was right. And so we embarked, crossing the thin strip connecting the land of people with the other world. Upon arriving, it appeared uninhabited. But following the narrow road, we came upon a small dwelling, likely a lone hermitage. It was obvious why a solitary monk would choose this place to fast and pray. We would like to have stayed, but Helios had begun his ride across the sky.

A bit further, a door welcomed, leading us to a small community of departed. What better place to lay one's head. Fearing we might disturb, we exited, following the path until a bend in the road revealed another entry. I suggested to Pa that we turn back, as this likely was the end of our walk.

"We've come this far, young man. Perhaps there's something beyond."

And Pa was right. Around every turn, there was the light of a new day dawning, and the light of a clear blue morning. Near the end of our walk, we looked back.

I nudged Pa "What was that place?"

Pa nudged back, "What if we hadn't stopped?"

Returning to the Pramataris, we gathered our things, ate in silence, and sipped the rich Greek coffee.

Recalling a line by the Hungarian writer Antal Szerb:

... while there is life there is always the chance something might happen,

I gave thanks for my life, my family, and for the second chance Pa's been given.

Not Enough Time

February 19

I can't speak for Pa, but I knew it would be this way.

A year ago, two years ago, when I was dreaming, thinking, beginning to plan, even then I knew I would only scratch the surface. Those who say, "you can't take it with you" are right of course. As are those who say, "you can't see it all," even in a lifetime. Whoever has?

Phileas Fogg, what did he hope for? Surely he knew he'd only have a bird's eye view.

Pa and I, we've been given twice the time, and yet it's not enough. There's not a place we've been that we wouldn't have stayed longer, or wished we'd seen more.

People write, "oh you must see … " Yes we should. And sometimes we do, but more often we can't. Father Time is always lurking, cajoling, dragging us along. And the muses, they whisper, "if you stay, what will you miss?"

It's a challenge, this balancing. You stay here, so you can't stay there. You see this, and you miss that. But that's life of course. Take yesterday. On the road from Monemvasia, we drive into the mountains, or so it seems. But we can't touch them. And the other road, how nice it would have been to follow it.

In Nafplio, where's there's so much, we got a taste. The old man, has he seen it all? We stay up to see the lights on the harbor, and wake early to see the sun rise on the old castle and the valley below. But we move on. And there are more decisions. This way, or that? And we take the one on the right, and the world opens up, and we discover Aylos BacíEIoS, stop for coffee, stay for breakfast, and meet Silio and his nephew, Theos.

But there are other roads, and had we taken one, and not the other, we might not have discovered the Corinth Canal, and learned of its architect and engineer, Istvan Turr. But we can't stay in Corinth, because the car must be returned, and we want to get to Athens and scratch the surface there.

Sgt. Pepper

February 20

We had an agenda, and knew the way, but got lost anyway, and happened upon a park, and being sunny as it was, were in no hurry, and lingered, and after a while had a sweet tooth, but were interrupted by a passing few, so we followed along, and there were more of them:

It was 20 years ago today

Travels with Pa

Sgt. Pepper taught the band to play

They've been going in and out of style

But they're guaranteed to raise a smile

So may I introduce to you,

Sgt. Pepper's Lonely Hearts Club Band.

It's wonderful to be here

It's certainly a thrill

You're such a lovely audience

We'd like to take you home with us

We'd love to take you home.

I don't really want to stop the show

But I thought you might like to know

That the singer's gonna sing a song

And he wants you all to sing along

So let me introduce to you ...

And we were transported, along with everyone else, and would like to have stayed, but the museum ...

Along the way, we stopped for more music, and dance, and freedom of expression, overseen by police and military. And in the near distance there was more music, and another band, with a parade following, and more freedom fighters, with military beside them. We thought of Plato, and his *Republic*. Even then, democracy was for the few.

Later than planned, we arrived, and returned to the roots of our civilization. Pa agreed that we learned a lot, but we can't get the band out of our head.

Ακρόπολη

February 21

The Acropolis. It's always there. Looking down on the city as if from Mt. Olympus. The crown jewel. We'd saved it for the last day.

But lying in bed before sunrise, Pa and I retraced our walk from the Archaeological Museum the afternoon before. We'd chosen a different route for the return home. Just to see. It was a post-apocalyptic walk. Buildings in decay, crumbling, providing refuge for addicts, prostitutes, the mentally ill and homeless. Out of respect, we took no photos.

Had the long economic downturn caused it, or were the roots much deeper? Could they be traced back to the earliest years of capitalism – or even before – to the time when family and village, somehow morphed into patriarchy, hierarchy, and the differentiation of classes?

But then the sun rose, and we threw open the curtains, and recalled a wonderful sentiment by Monica Baldwin:

Travels with Pa

The moment when first you wake in the morning is the most wonderful of the twenty-four hours. No matter how weary, there is the possibility that anything may happen.

Determined to beat the crowd, for there is a crowd even in February, we set out on a search for beauty, however it might manifest. Although we were in the "nice neighborhood," the one safe for tourists, we were occasionally reminded of the afternoon before.

Staying focused, we thought of Ann Frank who somehow remained focused the entirety of her young life.

I don't think of all the misery but of the beauty that still remains.

We continued on, taking the back way, delighting in the journey. After a time that seemed timeless, we were there, and heard the whisper of Abraham Heschel – scholar, mystic, peace activist – who at that end of his life was asked what he'd hoped for. To which the good rabbi replied:

Never once in my life did I ask God for success or wisdom or power or fame. I asked for wonder, and he gave it to me.

So we wandered about, not caring to read the history of the place, for that could be done later. Just to be there, that was enough.

I don't know if Simone Weil, the young French philosopher who died of starvation in protest of the Nazis, ever visited the Acropolis. But I'd like to believe that, even though she knew of its tainted history, she would have appreciated its beauty.

Everything beautiful has a mark of eternity.

At What Cost?

February 22

It's 6:30 Arabia Standard Time (AST) and the sun has set. Sayed, my seat mate, has dozed off after a stressful business week in Athens. He's an accountant with a small oil company based in Manama, Bahrain, his hometown. In less than an hour we'll touch down and his wife and three children will greet him. Sayed is well versed on the ways of the modern world, situated as he is at the crossroads between east and west. We talked earlier about China and the impact its one child policy is having on the global economy. About the fact that there is no money, just virtual digits somehow knitting us all together. And about the decline of Western Europe – the chaos there and in America.

He'd liked to visit New York City. "The chaos of that place would be nice for a week or two," he says, which led to a conversation about family. "There's no dating in Bahrain. When you meet a girl you like, you meet her family soon after to talk about marriage."

He showed us a scar above his left eyebrow. "I was nineteen, secretly having coffee with a girl I liked in a neighborhood far from ours. An uncle of hers saw us. An hour later I was pummeled by the uncle and three others. My family was angry for the longest time. I'd been taught never to break the rules."

As Sayed slept, Pa and I recalled our conversation with Kogas just before departing Athens. The day manager at the Palladian, Kogas, has a Masters in International Economics and taught us quite a bit about Greece, its politics, and its place in the modern world. Our conversation turned to antiquity and the amazing accomplishments of the ancient Greeks, accomplishments often not possible without the use of slave labor. He told us about Delos, an island in the Aegean Sea, long the center of slave trade for the Mediterranean world. Greeks and Romans both relied upon them, the Romans most, purchasing thousands to assist with its massive building projects – and to work in the homes of the privileged. The Colosseum used slaves in its construction, and for 350 years after to provide spectacle, along with gladiators, convicts, and prisoners. Historians believe as many as 400,000 died in the service of entertainment.

I mentioned to Kogas that I'd visited Machu Pichu where slave labor was instrumental in its construction. He lit up as he'll be visiting there in the spring. I suggested in preparation, that he read Pablo Neruda's epic poem. Therein, I told him, Neruda lays out the dilemma as only a poet can, that oftentimes beauty is made possible only by the sweat and blood of others:

I stare at the clothes and hands,

the carvings of water in a sonorous hollow,

the wall rubbed smooth by the touch of a face

that with my eyes gazed at the earthly lights,

that with my hands oiled the vanished

planks: because everything, clothes, skin, dishes ...

And tell me everything, tell chain by chain,

Travels with Pa

and link by link, and step by step;

sharpen the knives you kept hidden away,

thrust them into my breast, into my hands,

like a torrent of sunbursts,

an Amazon of buried jaguars,

and leave me cry: hours, days and years,

blind ages, stellar centuries.

On the drive to the airport, I couldn't help but think of America's use of slave labor – of its great sin – the White House, the Capital, Harvard, the Smithsonian, Wall Street.

In many ways I wondered, as did Neruda, *at what cost?*

CHAPTER FIVE
Dubai

The Mall

February 23

Many come to Dubai just for the beaches, and to shop at "The Mall", the world's largest. I didn't bring a swimsuit and neither Pa nor I are shoppers. But I needed hiking shorts for Nepal so we decided to go.

We took the Metro, state of the art, but somehow missed our stop. Overhead was a map and in five stops – the Mall of the Emirates – second best, but still. Not having had coffee, the line too long at breakfast, we stopped at the first possibility – the Carrefour city+. Sarah was out front. "Do you sell coffee," I inquired. "Of course, sir. Starbucks." Not my favorite, but we started to enter. "I'm sorry, sir, but you must stop here first." Sarah explained that I had to enter my name, email address, then swipe a credit card. I complied.

"You're all done, sir. After you finish, your receipt will be emailed." "Nothing else?" I ask. "Nothing else, sir."

They did have Starbucks, and many others. We chose a knockoff at half the price. Exiting, we stopped to thank Sarah. She's from Thailand, manages the shop, and is proud of the technology.

"It's the future, sir. Good for everyone."

Travels with Pa

The Mall is amazing, once you suspend all judgment. There are no Targets or Old Navy's, but if money is of no concern it can be heaven for a day. Most of the offerings are for women, or men buying gifts.

Lunch hour arrived. We chose an inviting little place with "outdoor seating". Offered the table of our choice, we were greeted by Jeffrey, the head waiter. I said I wanted to go lite. "What do you suggest?" "The chicken avocado on a warm croissant is a favorite." I trusted Jeffrey and ordered it with water and a side of fruit. Every five minutes or so Jeffrey stopped by, just to visit. He arrived in Dubai from the Philippines at 17 with his family. It's been twenty years and he's never left. "I have a wife and three children. We're treated well here."

I asked Jeffrey about Dubai customs.

"Never approach a woman without invitation, or take a photo of a woman without permission. Public displays of affection are frowned upon. Profanity isn't tolerated."

"Pretty simple," I said. "Pretty simple," he replied. "Otherwise, Dubai is very welcoming."

We met Jonathan as well. He filled our water glass. Also from the Philippines, he left 15 years ago and now has a family.

"My wife and I may go back when we're old," he says. "But not before. We have 4 children to raise."

Exiting, both men thanked us for our patronage.

We wandered, stopping at a small jewelry store where two young women greeted us, one from Kazakhstan, the other Vietnam.

Travels with Pa

We talked about their homes. "You would love Vietnam." "You would love Kazakhstan." They'll both return someday, but only after they've saved a lot.

We were then stopped by a young woman from Syria. She works for DAMAC selling "luxury apartments across Dubai." Describing the possibilities, "You can have a mid-level, 3 bedrooms with a swimming pool. Just 4 million in US dollars." I told her that if I win the lottery, I'll be back. She smiled.

Next door is a young man from Algeria. He works for a real estate company owned by the government. "For 1 million US dollars you can a have 1 bedroom – elite location – with 1100 sq feet." He showed us the possibilities.

"Swimming pool?" I ask. "No, but there's a sizable reflecting pool on the roof."

We talked about Algeria. He said I should visit. I told him I had wanted to but the Visa requirements are difficult. He shook his head. "Other countries make it difficult for us, so we do the same. Our laws are based on that." I thanked him for the conversation. "I'll be back if I win the lottery." He smiled.

Next, we met a pleasant young woman selling socks. They were on sale. "10 pair for 100." I tell her I'm traveling light. "1 pair is 24," she says. I tell her I've never spent that much on a pair of socks. But she has a beautiful smile and we allow her to show us the possibilities. We relented and bought a pair of "Popeyes."

I told her about Popeye the Sailor, that he had a cartoon show when I was a kid and ate spinach to stay strong. She loved the story, then showed me a pair of "Olive Oils." I told her I couldn't

Travels with Pa

spend 48, but thanked her.

A text arrived from CapitolOne. The foreign transaction was 6.41 in US currency. I returned, apologized, and bought the "Olive Oils."

We talked about Syria. She'll go back someday, after she travels.

"I have a boyfriend there. I love him so much. He honors my dream to travel and my need to gain confidence. He tells me all the time that when I'm done, and I'm confident, he will be there for me. I know he will," she says, and gets a little teary. I did too.

It was time to leave, but no shorts. But just then was an American Eagle store. We took a chance and were greeted by a young woman. "I need shorts, for hiking in Nepal." She escorted me to the Men's Dept. and explained my need to a young man. He promised to help as soon as he finished with another customer.

A second man approached and asked how he might assist. "I need shorts," I said. He showed me several pair, after which I settled on lightweight khakis. They're perfect.

I told him my name. "What's yours?" I ask. "Hari," he says, showing his name tag. Shaking his hand, "I'm from the United States." "I'm from Nepal," shaking mine. I told him I'm flying there on Saturday. "You must visit my hometown – Bhedetar. It's very beautiful." And he writes it down.

At the checkout, Hari needed assistance and calls for his supervisor. Van is from Myanmar. I tell him my name is Van Liew. He smiles. "My name is Van Lal."

We move on, the mall so extensive, we searched for a landmark.

Travels with Pa

A few steps and there it was.

Almost out, we stopped by Sarah's place but she wasn't in. We talked with the security guard – Kennedy from Uganda. "Like President Kennedy?" He smiled.

Finally we were out and sang an old Simon and Garfunkel song:

Someone told me

it's all happening at the zoo,

I do believe it,

I do believe it's true …

Back on the Metro every seat was taken. There was a sea of brown faces, every shade imaginable. We began to see nationalities. Rich diversity. Incredible beauty.

Halfway home there's an announcement:

"We are experiencing technical problems. Please be patient."

In no hurry, we decided to exit at the Emirate Towers. The train stops. It's rush hour.

"The gentleman wants to get off," says one near me.

"Please let the man off," says another.

And from the other side, "Please let him off."

"Please be careful, sir."

We're now in a different land.

Around the corner are the towers, and just across ,"The Museum of the Future." It was closed for an event, so we spoke with Raffi, a young security guard from Bangladesh. I asked if he knew the famous singer. Puzzled, I showed him a photo.

"Yes, yes. Very famous. I like him." And he beamed.

Tomorrow we're going to "The Mall." It has the world's largest aquarium.

It's A Long Way Up

February 24

We spent yesterday visiting "the Other Dubai" – walking the neighborhood, taking photos, having a wonderful Arabian lunch at an outdoor café. It was going to be a good blog.

The evening was set aside to visit the world's tallest building – the Burj Khalifa, 163 floors, 2,717 feet head to toe. Not a cheap ticket, but once in a lifetime. And a few extra dirhams bought us a ride past the 124th floor, to the 148th and the observation deck. Nearly sunset and a clear sky, we were awestruck.

I started taking photos like everyone else. Twenty-five, thirty or more before leaning to capture the little things on ground zero. I don't know why, but I raised my head, bumping it on a metal tube that keeps people from falling off. Reaching for the sore spot, I let go of my phone.

Time slowed as it floated like the feather in those early depictions of how gravity works. Of course there was nothing we could do but walk around as inconspicuously as possible, before

Travels with Pa

descending the 148 floors.

The Burj is connected to the Dubai Mall and soon enough we were at the Apple Store where Ahmed from Syria helped us with an iPhone 14. We talked about Syria, of course, and I shared the story of the young woman who sold us the Popeye socks.

"We Syrians are like that," Ahmed said. "We've suffered so much and yet maintain a belief that it will get better someday." He talked about his older sister, smuggled out of Syria to Germany eight years ago. "She had nothing when she arrived." Now she has a Master's Degree in Public Health and works with refugees.

Back at the hotel, we're on the hotel phone with T-Mobile for an hour and a half trying to get the iPhone activated. Just 477 dirhams. By the way, the photos from the day never made it to iCloud.

This morning Pa and I decided to go back to the neighborhood, stopping first at the Mall's "biggest in the world" aquarium.

A nice diversion. Following afternoon prayer, we had lamb chops again at the little restaurant. Grilled to perfection, they were worth twice the menu price. Waiting, we did some research and confirmed what we'd heard - that Dubai has a world-class surveillance system, blocks various social network platforms, and doesn't hesitate to jail to make a point.

No blog.

Back at the hotel we visited with Valerie from Zimbabwe who's getting her Master's Degree in Hospitality and Hotel Management from a university in South Africa. She submits her thesis in a week.

"My argument is that the poor treatment of service industry employees comes at considerable financial cost to shareholders. I'll do things different someday," she promised "I'm going to own a chain of hotels all around the world where everyone is treated like family."

Had I not bumped my head, we would not have met Valerie and Ahmed.

The Other Dubai

February 25

You live your life in a country and never really know it. Even less so when you travel, visiting a city for just three or four days. The typical visitor from the West lands at Dubai International, takes a taxi or private car to a five-star, then spends the remaining time at the Mall, the Beach, or the hotel's Dubai-sized pool. There's no need to go elsewhere.

But take the Metro and get off at a random stop, not Emirate Towers, the Financial Center, the Dubai Mall, or those serving the quiet neighborhoods, and you're likely to stumble on "The Other Dubai." The Dubai where the workers who serve the privileged live and raise their families. I suppose Dubai is like Silicon Valley in that respect.

As luck would have it, Pa and I hopped off at one of the "other stations." Underground, it looked like the others, but stepping outside we were in a land far different from the concrete wonderland a few Metro stops away. It's not a ghetto, but it's not the suburbs. Life is raw, and more alive in its immediacy. The restaurant owner and shopkeeper live next door or upstairs from their customers. The men, come prayer time, congregate together.

And beyond that Dubai, is another. The one where non-Arabs live. Those who clean hotel rooms and restrooms, and scrub the floors at fancy restaurants and the Mall. They come from India, Pakistan, Nepal, and Bangladesh on temporary visas that require them to ride the carousel of go home, return, go home, return, go home when you're no longer needed.

On the shuttle to the airport the driver asked whether I was departing from Terminal 1 or Terminal 3. I didn't know so I looked at my confirmation email. No mention of it. I Googled FlyDubai and learned that most flights are out of Terminal 3. Pulling up, I checked our boarding pass. Terminal 2. I asked the driver if I could walk. I could not. I'd have to take a bus or taxi. Pa and I walked about clueless, until a young man approached.

"Where are you going, sir?"

"Terminal 2," I replied. "Can I walk?"

"You cannot, sir. You need to take the bus. The taxi is too expensive."

He asked if I had a Metro card. I told him I gave it to the young man at the hotel who cleaned my room.

"Follow me."

I told him I didn't have money to pay him, but I'd figure it out.

"No worry, sir."

He led us to the Metro kiosk where I purchased a card sufficient for the bus. Returning to the spot where he found us, he asked, "What time does your flight depart?"

"10:20," I responded.

"You won't make it, sir. Not enough time. You need to take a taxi."

He grabbed my bag and we followed, getting to know each other on the way.

Tony is from Ghana, where he learned to weld pipelines for the oil fields. A "recruiter" convinced him to travel to Dubai, a trip that cost Tony all his savings. There was no job when he arrived. Tony's been in Dubai for three years and can't get out. He's had other jobs, but like so many others, gets laid off without notice.

I remembered that I had $400 in 50s and 20s in an envelope tucked deep in my backpack. We stopped, I gave him a twenty, then we walked on.

Tony sleeps in a small room with four bunk beds, three high, spending his nights on the top of one as it's the cheapest. The men in his room pool their money for groceries and take turns preparing meals. Every morning Tony is at the airport at 7:00 to see who he can help. For every dollar he earns, two are sent to his parents and three sisters.

Tony found us a taxi, introducing us to his friend Ahamad from Pakistan. Tony and I shake hands and I give him a fifty. There was nothing else I could do.

On the way to Terminal 2, Ahamad opens up. "Too much money here. Too much greed. We do all the work yet they treat us like we're nothing." The fare was $6.40. I gave Ahamad a twenty. There was nothing else I could do.

I get to my gate. A sea of brown faces. Terminal 2, I learn, is for "regional flights" on the old planes to India, Pakistan, Nepal, and Bangladesh.

The hotel shuttle driver was an Arab gentleman. He had no reason to tell me about Terminal 2. I'm a white man from the West.

CHAPTER SIX
Nepal

Swagat

February 26

Prior to leaving home, I'd convinced Pa that we should visit Nepal, and for an extended period. He knew little of the country other than the 1953 summit of Everest by Sir Edmund Hillary and Tenzing Norgay. I knew little more, aside from what I'd gathered from conversations with a few who'd visited, and from reading Krakauer's *Into Thin Air*. I told Pa about the book, promising we wouldn't be attempting a summit.

We decided that Kathmandu would be our first stop, since we'd be landing at its international airport, and to experience the chaotic city before moving on. Beyond the ten days we'd booked at Swagat Homestay, we had no plans. We chose the Swagat because Sugat and his wife, the owners, live on the premises with their two young children, and because it's in a "quiet" neighborhood.

The Swagat is a welcoming place, the word meaning the same in Nepalese, situated in a cluster of homes with our room facing north. At breakfast - eggs, toast, a banana, and Nepalese black tea - we told Sugat we thought we'd stay close to home the first day, easing slowly into the city. He thought that was a good plan. After a conversation with a retired couple from the Netherlands, one that Pa thoroughly enjoyed, we set out.

For the Nepalese, according to Sugat, Friday and Saturday are the weekend, the intensity of the city half the remaining five. Come Sunday morning, the week begins again, with kids in school and their parents back to work. With that in mind, we started shortly after sunrise.

It was quiet as promised, the day just beginning for most. We'd learned from the Dutch couple that the Nepalese customarily sleep in, having little compulsion to rise at the crack of dawn. It appeared that way as we strolled through back streets just coming to life.

Dutch Man Sings Bocelli in Nepal

February 27

Back home, Thijs Hannen is a chief archivist for the government, the first in the Netherlands to introduce digital archiving. In his spare time, he makes music. Thijs and his partner, Anjelica, sponsored a university student from Nepal a few years ago. The young woman frequently encouraged them to visit her country. They promised to do so if and when she got married. The two-day event took place a month ago. Since then, Thijs and Anjelica have been exploring, ending up in Kathmandu and at Swagat Homestay ten days ago.

Thijs is classically trained and performs on a number of instruments. During COVID, he fell in love with opera. Now it's his first love, so much so that he's composing a mini-opera on

Travels with Pa

Mozart's life. When Sugat learned of Thijs' passion, the two put together an evening of music at Sugat's new restaurant, the Jacaranda, to which Pa and I were invited. Despite the rain and a power outage, it was a wonderful evening. Dinner preceded the entertainment, during which I had a platter of deep-fried momos, a kind of dumpling at the top of the list of Nepalese favorites.

Then the concert began. Thijs started with a few favorites, *Hallelujah* included. Anjelica was enamored, and nearly everyone sang along. A traditional Nepalese song was next, followed by opera, Mozart, Wagner, Pavarotti. Near the end, Thijs changed into Nepalese attire and played the Nepalese anthem. At my request, he closed with Andrea Bocelli's *Time to Say Goodbye*, in Italian. It was a hit.

After everyone had left, Pa and I visited with Thijs, Anjelica, Sugat, Roshani, and Giovanni (a young man from France). It was the best evening for Pa and me since leaving home.

This morning, Thijs had an engagement at a school near Swagat, attended by 200 students and supported by several individuals and organizations. Thijs had previously met with the principal and offered to teach a class. Today was the day.

Thijs and the students started with a traditional Dutch tune, followed by a Japanese children's song. The finale was Nepal's national anthem, supported by students on traditional drums:

Afterwards, while Thijs spoke with the principal, Roshani, and two teachers, Pa and I met with a few of the students and talked about singing.

Waking Up

February 28

Just our third day, but we were getting acclimated. Slowly, we had extended our walks in length and in scope. This morning, Pa and I headed out to the main street, the one each of the little neighborhoods feeds into, like tributaries into a great river. We'd been out there before, but only to have coffee. This morning, we took in the sights.

At that early hour, traffic was light, and the businesses that have defined spaces had yet to open. Yet business had started. Up and down the street, fruits and vegetables were being sold by mini markets, the principal providers of food for the day.

After a time, we stopped for coffee at the place we visited the day before. They have a great cappuccino. A little pricey by neighborhood standards, but worth it. Relaxing in easy chairs, we took it all in.

In the time during which we sipped and watched, other businesses opened their doors, and the day was on. Ten minutes later we arrived at our landmark and turned left for Sugat's place. Along the way there had been others, taking it all in.

Untethered

March 1

It's 4:30. Absolute silence. No roosters crowing or small feathered ones calling to friends and neighbors. Evan has yet to assert his three-year-old self, and not a motorcycle nearby. I prefer to sleep in, but I've been sorting through something the past hour and need to process. Nikos Kazantzakis, in his autobiography *Report to Greco*, mused that he couldn't think without a pen in his hand. It's like that.

I've been noticing over the past few weeks what I initially labeled "a shift." But it's not that. It's more of a phenomenon. A different way of being in the world. A different way the mind is in the world. Someone wrote a book entitled *The Untethered Soul*. Perhaps it's like that.

There are the obvious things. Home is halfway 'round the world. There's no work to attend to. No radios in the car or televisions nearby. Spotify, Audible.com, even Kindle hold little interest. The *New York Times* app seems irrelevant. It's the mind bumping up against the world without a buffer or intermediary to soften, intervene, or protect.

Years ago, Shunryu Suzuki wrote *Zen Mind, Beginner's Mind*. It's like that. Every day, everything is new. There are no boxes within which to neatly store observations and interactions. No patterns constructed on past experience to rely upon. *Be Here Now*, Ram Dass taught. It's like that.

And it just happens. There's no effort, no process, no method. The will plays no part in it, nor does the "little self" have a say in it. It's the product of stripping down, of being stripped down. Everything in a backpack, moving from one room to the next, one culture to the next, it all contributes. And then there's the "just being out there."

In some ways, Kathmandu is the culmination. The West appears to have little influence here. It probably does, but it's not apparent. And everything seems to happen in plain sight. Stuff happens behind closed doors, no doubt. How could it not? Otherwise there'd be no little ones running around. But so much of the business of daily life is on the street. And you grow accustomed to it.

Take the traffic here. I had some preparation, the cities that came before, particularly in Italy and Greece. But they weren't like this. The first day I could feel it in my stomach, unaccustomed to this level of chaos. But by yesterday, it just was.

There's a dance taking place.

A Goat Story

March 2

There's a story about a goat. But we'll get to that later. It's best to start at the beginning of the day.

A new guest arrived from Germany. I've forgotten his name already. He's a nurse, a very nice fellow, and had just completed a lengthy Himalayan trek. Oh to be young again. Anyway, at breakfast, Sugat, the German, Pa, and I had a stimulating conversation, most of it centering on death and dying. The German knows a lot about both, having spent a long time as a hospice nurse. I shared Karen's story, how she chose the date and time to move on, with the aid of a medication prescribed by her physician. Germany isn't there yet, and Nepal is years away. Sugat says the funeral industry is a huge obstacle.

So we talked about death, how the elderly are treated, mistreated, how they're isolated, and how there was a time when generations lived under the same roof. We talked about the passing on of real estate and the archaic laws that often result in unfairness. It was a good conversation.

After breakfast, Rama, Sugat's trusted taxi driver, picked me up. I've ridden with him on four occasions, always arriving at my destination unscathed. Rama is fearless, navigating Kathmandu traffic with great courage. I have a 15-minute video from yesterday's adventure but hesitate to share it. Anyway, we arrived without incident, although Pa confided later that there were a few times he thought he might be returning home earlier than planned.

Our meeting was with Sugat's brother-in-law, Ujjwal Amatya, the country representative for Mission East. Tomorrow we'll talk about his work.

On the drive back, we stopped at the river's edge. Across the way is a slum that stretches up and down the opposite bank. The land is owned by the government, and five thousand live there. There are wealthy individuals who own land there, too, just to have it. And somehow, the Nepalese Mafia is involved. Ujjwal clued us in. The Mafia's principal activity is corrupt land deals, but it engages in sex trafficking as well, taking young girls from the mountains and selling them in Dubai. Having been there, we weren't surprised to hear that. By the way, the Nepalese Communist Party is in control now, though tenuously, having barely defeated the Congress Party in the last election. And there are

Travels with Pa

Chinese spies in Durbar Square. I'll be going there today.

After returning to Sugat's place, Pa and I left again to do some banking. Twice the ATM machine malfunctioned. A very nice young man did his best to fix it. Unsuccessful, he gave us directions to Citizens Bank where we withdrew 25,000 rupees, $189.39 in US currency at the time of the transaction. Next to Citizens is the British Coffee School, which we'd visited earlier in the week. Saru, the senior student, was our server. We talked about his dream to go to the United States and work for Starbucks. He asked my opinion on whether it's better to use slang or formal English. We had a good conversation and, afterward, met with other students. Pa and I enjoyed the visit very much.

Early evening we went looking for dinner, deciding on a little Indian place a mile from home. There was a menu, but just two items were being served, Chicken Biryani and Goat Biryani. We almost went with the goat, then remembered the story.

By the way, the Chicken Biryani was wonderful, and the sweet dessert served with it. Oh my. All for $3.18, a bottle of water included.

So the goat story.

Sugat had told me about a guest he'd once had from Austria. "The kindest man I've ever met," he said. One day the man showed up with a goat wearing a jacket. Sugat asked questions. Turns out the Austrian had happened upon a butcher shop where the goat was about to be executed. That couldn't happen. So the goat was purchased for 300 euros. The jacket came later.

So the goat and the kind man arrive at Swagat Home Stay. Sugat tells them, as much as he'd like to help, there's no room in the inn for the goat. But he has a friend, a very conscientious farmer. The farmer agrees to take the goat in. In the meantime, Evan, Sugat and Roshani's little boy, becomes attached to the goat. And the goat to Evan.

The next day Rama arrived, and the Austrian and goat got in. There were tears, but Mom and Dad assured Evan the goat was going to a very good home.

And that's the only goat story I know.

In Search of Hanuman Dhoka

March 3

Before we left home, I downloaded a World Clock to keep track of the time changes. When Pa and I arrived in Nepal, we added "Kathmandu" to the list of cities, and were quite surprised. It appeared that when it's the top of the hour back home, or in other cities we'd visited or would visit, Kathmandu was 15 minutes off. Quite an oddity. It was particularly bothersome to Pa, always punctual as he is. For me, I was certain some sense could be made of it, and that any Nepalese could explain the logic.

On the second day, I queried Sugat and showed him the clock. He was befuddled, never having known of the discrepancy. The following day I spoke with a friend of Sugat's. Equal consternation. Yesterday I visited Trevini School again. The principal, Lama Sir, puzzled. This morning I mentioned it to Roshani. For the first time, a glimmer of recognition. "I think it has something to do with India," she said.

So we Googled, of course, and the search turned up a 2003 *Nepali Times* article that attempts to explain it.

When Westerners arrived, they brought global time zones, which used, and still use, the Greenwich Meridian as zero and measure 24 standard meridians on longitudes 15 degrees apart. It wasn't until 1956, however, that the Nepalese first set their watches to Nepal Standard Time, with the meridian at Mt. Gauri Shankar, 100 km east of Kathmandu.

By doing so, a Nepalese clock or watch would be 10 minutes ahead of India, which had used the longitude that passed through Calcutta. When India switched its meridian to Hyderabad in 1971, there were then four degrees of separation, putting Nepal 15 minutes ahead of its neighbor to the south.

Very interesting, and Pa agrees there's a certain logic to it. But more interesting is how the Nepalese kept time before Westerners arrived.

In the Malla period, if you wanted to know the exact time in Kathmandu, you'd go to a pond near Hanuman Dhoka, a complex of structures that to this day includes the Royal Palace of the Malla kings. Once there, an official would tell you how many *pala* had submerged since dawn. Each *pala* had a tiny hole and would fill up in exactly 24 minutes.

We're not quite sure of the logic of that, but it's got me thinking about getting a fishpond when we return home. Anyway, the whole thing prompted us to visit Hanuman Dhoka, which includes one of the three Durbar Squares in central Kathmandu.

Following breakfast, we were off. The directions on Google Maps were straightforward, until we arrived at Shankhadar Park and were directed to pass through it to the other side. We gladly paid the entry fee (100 rupees / $0.76 USD) and slowly made our way through. After crossing the busiest intersection we'd yet encountered, we ended up in the outside waiting area of Bir Hospital's 200-bed Emergency and Trauma Centre. We looked around a bit, exited on the far side, and entered Thamel, the heart of tourist shopping in Kathmandu.

The back streets and alleys were interesting, and there were other sights as well, but we slowly extricated ourselves and arrived at the complex. Quite a sight, numerous sights, actually. At one point we happened upon the home of the *Kumari*, the "living goddess." Entering, we learned she'd be appearing soon and a ritual would begin. Not knowing the immediacy of "soon," we approached the exit, only to discover the arrival of the keepers of the ritual. Whatever was supposed to happen, happened outside, and a few minutes later we were following a small procession on its way somewhere else.

After a time, we turned back and followed a different crowd, stopping at one holy place after another, including those damaged in the 2015 earthquake.

A Bump Along the Way

March 4

When we visited the school the other evening, Pa and I briefly

Travels with Pa

made the acquaintance of Dawa Lama. An older gentleman and very wise. We'll talk about Lama Sir in a few days, but I bring him up now as he's a philosopher of sorts. In sharing his reading interests, I knew he could direct us to a good English bookstore. And he did.

The Mandala Book Point is on the main road, not far from Hanuman Dhoka, if you know the way. Pa and I were certain we did. Walking along, nodding to folks, we marveled at how the Nepalese navigate life. There's potential peril in such walking, however. One is prone to not take care of one's own business. Something can happen. Some unintended event might occur. And so it did.

We'd just approached a side street, perhaps an undeserving label, about to merge with the main artery. The surface was uneven. It's fair to say it wasn't pavement at all. Looking around, as we so often do, we failed to notice what was underfoot, stumbled, and bumped into a young woman. No damage was done, but the lack of care deserved an apology. And we did, readily. The young woman responded with the most beautiful smile. Accepting our apology, she inquired as to my home country. In no apparent hurry, she asked more questions before calling to her classmates a short distance ahead. Within seconds, the three of us were united with the three of them and a conversation ensued. A polite one, and all at once. The three were so much like the young woman we'd bumped, they easily could be sisters. And they are, in a non-biological way.

Their enthusiasm for life was infectious. Now in college, one day they'll make a big difference in the world. They're certain of it. Men won't out-compete them, because they'll work harder and smarter. All four want to study abroad, returning with good ideas and practices that will aid their country.

At the risk of imposing, I asked if I might take their photo. "Of course!" they shouted in unison, Jyoti Gaihre, Prasanna Bhattarai, Nilima Kharel, and Unisha. They then insisted I be included. Resisting, Nilima took my phone and completed the selfie. Pa then suggested we do a short video so the world will know what kind of women they are.

We could have stayed, but all four had studying to do. Proceeding in the same direction, two parted company after a short time; the remaining two insisted they get us closer to our destination. Arriving at the crossover, they took the right and we the left. We were in Thamel, but an unfamiliar area. Having forgotten about Google Maps, we proceeded through the maze, certain we'd recognize landmarks. But the shops were unknown to us. We were in the Asian Bazaar, a delightful place. And not just shops, little temples too.

After a time, the maze turned quiet, and we thought it best to consult Google. The Mandala was not far off. And so it was, across the street. I took a step into the traffic, but Pa would have none of it. Tugging at my sleeve, he spoke rather tersely:

"Young man, always remember that caution is the better part of valor."

Pa, always the Dutchman. But he was right, of course. So we proceeded to the overpass, crossed over, walked an equal distance back, and arrived. Shortly after, Siddhartha introduced himself and assigned his associate, Hiranjan, to assist. There were many possibilities, but we ultimately purchased an important book by an influential Nepalese writer.

We then visited, about Buddhism, capitalism, communism, the strengths and weaknesses of the Nepalese people, about the challenges ahead. With other customers waiting, Pa and I thanked the kind men, having learned a lot.

On the return to Swagat Home Stay, we stopped for a bubble tea and made the acquaintance of Dawa Tsering. After serving us a delicious chocolate tea, we learned that Dawa is finishing his undergraduate work in business and will move to France soon to begin his MBA. Following the completion of his studies, he'll enter the French Foreign Legion.

"Every young man needs an adventure," he told us.

He will then return to Nepal and open a chain of bubble tea shops all over the country.

I have no doubt he will.

On the Road to Khokana

March 5

Pa and I had planned to visit the tea fields near Bhotechaur, an hour north of Kathmandu. But I woke with intestinal discomfort and informed Sugat we'd have to cancel with Ram. Later, though, I was feeling better, and Pa agreed that we might visit someplace closer to home.

Khokana is a traditional Newar village 10 kilometers to the

Travels with Pa

south, a reasonable distance, given my needs. Sugat called Ram back, and we were on the road to Khokana by ten. Ram, as noted earlier, is quite trustworthy and knows his way around Kathmandu as well as I know my own neighborhood. Twenty minutes into our journey, however, it was apparent that he'd never been to Khokana. Once, twice, then a third time, he stopped to inquire about its whereabouts. I consulted Google Maps as well. Ten minutes passed, and we were close. Another ten minutes, and it was just beyond a cluster of buildings we were passing through.

A problem arose, however, when we came upon a truck that blocked our passage. Ram attempted to negotiate, but to no avail. Backing up, we were helped by locals. Once pointed in the direction from which we had come, Ram inquired again about Khokana's location. A nice fellow pointed straight ahead, then left.

Soon we were on a dirt road that ended abruptly. There was no going forward. Ram preferred to stay with his car, while I set out on foot in search of Khokana.

It was a beautiful walk, one I would have chosen had I known about it. But several minutes passed and Khokana was nowhere in sight. Just to our right, a gate was open, and Pa suggested we ask for directions. Looking around, a young man appeared, introduced himself as Samiir, and asked if I was hungry. Not particularly, but I agreed to see the menu. Fresh fish was listed, which sounded good to both of us.

Samiir came from behind the counter and gestured that we follow. Once outside, he pointed into a tank, suggesting a choice be made. Intrigued, I pointed at the largest. A struggle ensued, but Samiir prevailed. Not long after, lunch was being prepared.

To pass the time, I ordered hookah, knowing Pa wouldn't participate. As an appetizer, Samiir offered a bowl of seasoned corn. Delicious. Between puffs of apple and bites of corn, we learned about Samiir. He's from Bandipur, six hours by bus to the west, depending on road conditions. Pa and I happen to have a 7 AM ticket for Bandipur the next day. Back home, Samiir lives with his family and spends spare time on TikTok. With great pride, he showed us video snippets, his brother dancing, his sister singing.

"He's very famous on TikTok," Samiir informed us.

Just then, our meal arrived. Quite delicious. We ate, drank, and puffed slowly until noticing the time. Having promised Ram we'd return by one, we needed to be on our way. After thanking Samiir and settling up, I inquired if he knew of Khokana.

"Of course," he said. "It's up there, on top of the hill," pointing to the cluster of buildings we had visited with Ram.

On our walk back, lunch was over for the locals and there was work to be done. One o'clock arrived and Ram was waiting, as promised.

Postscript – Khokana.

It's a lovely village, sprucing itself up as it awaits word on its UNESCO application. After our tour, we sat, reveling in the day, and sharing stories about goats.

Travels with Pa

Kapan

March 6

Researching Kathmandu, I learned of Kapan. Perched high on a hill overlooking the city, the monastery is home to several hundred Tibetan Buddhist monks.

I'd forgotten about Kapan until Pa said he needed some quiet time. I knew what he meant, an afternoon to recharge, to shake off the constancy of street life. Sugat gave Ram a call, and within minutes he arrived. Communicating our needs as best we could, Ram offered assurance that he could get us there. It's not a long drive, and Ram did well, until the very end, when a fork in the road confused him. He suggested left. Pa and I, the opposite. Being the paying customers, we prevailed. In the end, however, either choice would have got us there.

Anyway, Ram climbed the very steep hill with his noble steed, arriving at the point beyond which no vehicles are allowed. From there, a gravel path led to a large gate, and to the left, a small opening, with a sign overhead: NO ENTRY. We proceeded with caution until a gatekeeper, perhaps on break, barked:

"There is no entry. You must go to the right."

We did, finding a well-trod path upon which we embarked. It wasn't a difficult path, though some exertion was required. That seemed right and proper. It should not have been easy to reach our destination. Perhaps that was by design, intended to discourage the unworthy, or at least the casual observer.

Moving on, however, it became clear that the path itself was not the challenge, but the fact that it clung precipitously to the side of a steep hillside.

But Pa, having no fear of death, urged me on. All in all, it was a pleasant stroll, preparatory for what was to come. After a time, one of those times when it appears there is no time, we arrived at a second gate and spoke with a second gatekeeper. Far more welcoming than the first, he urged us to enter and pointed up the hill, an ascent that proved taxing. But again, one must earn the right to visit such places.

Rounding what turned out to be the final bend, we arrived. And just arriving could have been enough. But Pa urged us on, demonstrating once again his innate curiosity. Proceeding silently, we explored, marveling at how the human heart can manifest itself in architecture and art. At least once in our lives we find ourselves in a place, made by the hand of God or of man, so sublime that whatever happens after is of little significance.

On the drive to Kapan, we were hopeful that we'd be allowed within the monastery's walls. That was no longer necessary. Walking slowly, paying attention, listening to the birds chirping and the music of children at play far in the distance, that was enough. But out of nowhere, it seemed, a monk appeared at our side. Offering our respect, we found he pointed to a door. Unlocking it, he gestured that we follow. Inside was a narrow vestibule and a second door, which he also unlocked. We removed our shoes and followed.

And there we were, in the great hall, the sanctuary, where boys and men are molded into monks on the path. We asked if we could stay. Pasangdorjee, our guide, nodded. In awe, we slowly began to follow the stories unfolding well above eye level. We then approached the altar to the left and inquired of our guide about the walls on either side of the altar.

"Our prayer books," he said.

We asked if we might sit and pray. He nodded and laid down a meditation mat. All the while, the young monk waited with the greatest patience.

Knowing the monastery would soon close, we thanked our guide and exited through the doors from which we'd come, only to find young monks at play on the sunny afternoon.

Quietly, we bid farewell, our way back having acquired a luminescence.

Pa and I, at the same instant, recalled Eliot…

We shall not cease from exploration

And the end of all our exploring

Will be to arrive where we started

And know the place for the first time…

The Long Haul

March 7

It wasn't an issue for Pa, but I needed to prepare. No food after lunch the day before. No fluids after 6 p.m. I was faithful to the plan, much to my later relief.

Pa and I were up by five. Ram arrived punctually at six, delivering us to the bus stop at 6:20. On board soon after, we were on our way by seven. In the interval between 6:40 and departure, a French woman and a British fellow had a bit of a tiff. Each insisted they were ticketed for seat 1. The French woman eventually produced documentary evidence to prove her case, relegating the British fellow to seat 3. Pa and I knew all along we had been assigned seat 2. A good thing, we reflected, should future negotiations become necessary.

In the early going, the British fellow – Barry - was a bit taciturn. Allowing him the benefit, I attributed it to a long-standing animosity, perhaps he'd been married to a French woman.

It takes a good while to get out of Kathmandu, at least an hour this morning. But eventually, we were on the open road, and Barry opened up.

"Are you ticketed for the long haul?" he inquired.

Uncertain as to his meaning, I told him we had a ticket for Pokhara but were getting off at Bandipur.

"Good thing," he said. "If all goes well, it's 9–10 hours to Pokhara. Other days it might be 11 or more. If there's a landslide, you won't make it at all."

The British aren't disposed to sugarcoating.

Turning to Google Maps:

Kathmandu > Pokhara: 200 km / 125 miles.

Oh my. Better to take a slow boat to China.

Travels with Pa

Kathmandu > Bandipur: 150 km / 94 miles.

Oh boy. We were in for a long haul.

Barry turned out to be quite pleasant, and at two hours we made our first stop. A simple place with simple food. Having disciplined myself, and aware of the general workings of my digestive system, I purchased a potato ball, a side of cabbage, and some sort of breakfast sandwich. The sandwich was soon discarded, but the remaining two were quite tasty.

Back on the road, the drive was pleasant, reaching speeds of 40 mph.

Barry and I talked about the big European football clubs - how Russian, Saudi, and American interests now own the best teams, the widespread corruption, and the lack of player loyalty.

"I know professional sport in America has its flaws," he said, "but there's much it has over us."

We also spoke about Nepal. He's been coming for 45 years. Retired now, Barry was an electrical contractor in London, returning every winter now to Nepal for two months.

Between her cat naps, I spoke with the French woman as well. Though she never volunteered her name, there's much to admire. About the same age as Barry, mid-sixties my guess, she's an architect from Paris who first came to Nepal after the earthquake. Off and on for two years she helped with reconstruction efforts. Now she lives full-time in a village 45 minutes west of Pokhara, working with women engaged in small sustainability projects.

At eleven o'clock it was time for a second stop. Somewhat of an upgrade, the Blue Heaven, a pleasant place, served a vegan buffet for 300 rupees and one with meat for 450. It was quite nice.

Back on the road we did well, until we didn't, finally getting a sense of the "long haul." After numerous stops and starts, with speeds the average bicyclist would exceed, the call came:

BANDIPUR

And just like that, we were at the stop, with Bandipur 10 km away and up the side of a mountain. We considered a minibus at first, but there being no announced departure time, we hailed a taxi and arrived at the charming mountain town 30 minutes later.

Six and a half hours door to door. Perhaps a record.

Bandipur

March 8

Monday was *Holi*, the Festival of Colours day. Had we known before planning our visit to Bandipur, we would have remained another day in Kathmandu. Roshani had asked more than once, "will you be here Monday?" She'd then explain the day's importance - the victory of good over evil, the arrival of spring, the unity of all peoples.

Originally a festival day for Hindus alone, Nepalese throughout the country now celebrate it, but with no greater passion than in Kathmandu according to Roshani.

We carried on, though, arriving in Bandipur in the afternoon. After cleaning up and resting, we went out to explore the Newar hilltop town, the remaining daylight permitting - but not before receiving a photo from Sugat, with Roshani and our friend Marco. Having come to know Sugat, we believe he was rubbing it in a bit.

People come to Bandipur for many reasons, its stunning views among them. Walking a short distance from the Hotel Aagamon, we passed the first of several historic Newari homes, then stopped to admire some youthful revelers. After dinner we were out again. It was quiet, with the exception of four happy lads not ready to call it a day.

The next morning at breakfast, Imal taught us to make traditional masala tea:

- cardamom
- clove
- ground peppercorn
- black loose leaf tea
- milk
- sugar

brought to a boil, then strained. If I could get it everywhere, I'd never drink coffee again.

By breakfast's end, Bandipur was waking up and ready for the day - walking to school, or out for a stroll, in their shops or repairing the road, or just hanging with mom.

Bandipur is one of those places you didn't know existed, but finding it, you never forget it.

The Protectors

March 9

There was an early morning haze over the mountains forecasting rain, or perhaps change of some other kind.

At breakfast, Shasi, who owns and operates Hotel Aagaman with her husband Rudra, told us she'd be leaving for Kathmandu airport at ten with their daughter, who will soon begin her university studies in Melbourne.

In just a day we'd grown fond of Shasi and Rudra, admiring their tenacity. Until a year ago, the couple ran a photocopy business in Kathmandu, which they'd started in 2010. All the while they saved for their dream: to move to Bandipur and open a hotel. It was the right move, and travelers passing through have rewarded their hard work.

Before leaving, Shasi made arrangements for Lok to pick us up for the drive to Pokhara.

"He's as good a driver as you will ever find," she told us. "He's a Gurkha. They're fearless."

After Shasi departed, and while waiting for Lok, Rudra educated us on the Gurkha.

"They're a hill people, originating not far from here. I've been told the Gurkha take their name from a medieval Hindu warrior-saint, Guru Gorakhnath, the word derived from *Goraksha*, 'Protector.'"

I asked Rudra his opinion of Lok.

"He's a Gurkha through and through. Protectors of Nepal for centuries, they fought off India's attempts to take us over. Now they fight in our army, the Indian Army, the British Army, and with UN Peacekeeping Forces. Do you know what they say about the Gurkhas?"

We didn't, of course.

"If a man says he's not afraid of dying, he is either lying or he's a Gurkha."

In the moment, we weren't sure if that's a good thing or not on the road to Pokhara.

Shortly after, Lok arrived behind the wheel of a little Suzuki. We learned on the drive that Lok had purchased it new in India a few months prior, having saved for five years.

We immediately liked this Gurkha, and regret not getting his photo. Knowing that he's descended from a long line of Gurkha fighters, we felt comfortable seated next to him.

It was a pleasant enough ride on the highway China is building, Lok taking on every obstacle with skill and grace. Three years into the massive project, in two more a four-lane highway will connect Kathmandu with Pokhara. Though some in Nepal have expressed concern about the patronage, thousands of Nepalese will benefit from the ease of travel.

Lok is a man of few words, but he opened up at times when the driving allowed it. He was never a soldier, although his father was, fighting in the Indian army. After his father was killed, Lok took to driving a taxi to support the family. About to turn fifty, that was thirty-five years ago. Until recently, he drove in Pokhara, but then he met a good woman and they moved to Bandipur. The couple's eight-year-old son is in school full-time.

"The love of my life," Lok told us.

Forty-five minutes earlier than expected, we arrived at the Hotel Mountain Villa. After saying our good-byes, we were greeted by Sugat's good friend, Probin. Later we went for a stroll, after which Probin treated us with hot lemon juice and ginger. Sipping on the tangy sweet tea, Pa and I reflected on our brief time with Lok.

"Though he was never a soldier," Pa said, "there's no doubt he would have been a fine one."

Mr. Vishnu

March 10

Shortly after 7, and before Pa and I had a chance to stretch, Probin yelled up, "Fred, I've got your masala tea." A minute later he was at the door with a steamy glass of the rich milky brew. Thirty minutes passed and Probin yelled up again, "Fred, I've got your breakfast." Before we could exit the bathroom, it was on the table next to the door and he was gone. We're going to have to talk with Sugat about adding room service to his list of offerings.

The tea was excellent, as was the breakfast, and by 8 we were out the door anticipating a good day. Looking up and down the street in search of the lake, we looked up as well. And there was Annapurna, at 26,545 ft, number 10 on the list of the world's highest peaks.

It was going to be a good day.

Pa suggested we walk downhill as the lake would most likely be there. I would have concluded the same if given more time. So I followed Pa's lead and within a minute or two we concluded that there was a different feel to Pokhara. The pace is slower. The traffic so minimal, you can stand in the middle of the street without taking your life in your hands. Even the cows know that. And so it was when we arrived at the lake, a few gentlemen visiting casually with no apparent need to hurry.

Pa and I walked to the lake's edge. Oh my. And to our right, long multi-colored boats the likes of which neither of us had ever seen. Considering a ride, walking back we were met by a little man:

"I'm Mr. Vishnu. How can I help?"

I told him I was interested in a boat ride, perhaps later in the afternoon when the sun was low in the sky.

"That's a good time," said Mr. Vishnu. "I suggest five o'clock."

I asked who our pilot would be.

Travels with Pa

"I will, sir. You will find me quite capable."

Pa whispered, "He's a good man." So we shook on it.

Walking back up the hill, we were stopped by the smell of coffee. On the menu was café mocha, another brew I have a great fondness for. Our barista was Basmaya, a capable young lady. As we were settling up, I introduced myself and she did the same. Not quite grasping her full name, I asked if she might spell it out. She obliged.

"Oh, you're a Gurung, a very courageous people," knowing the Gurung are one of the main Gurkha tribes.

She beamed, "Yes we are. My father, and my father's father fought in the Indian army. And before them, others fought against the Indians."

It's a small world.

Afternoon came and we were back at the lake with Mr. Vishnu pushing us off. Pa was right. Mr. Vishnu is a good man having lived quite a life. His father was a porter on the trekking circuit. When Mr. Vishnu turned 16 he joined his father. For thirty years he shouldered loads up to sixty pounds, on treks 25 days and longer, and at altitudes as high as 24,000 feet. Finally he accomplished what his father did not. He became a guide leading expeditions with men and women from around the world.

Mr. Vishnu learned much about the modern way of things, some of which he admired and some he had no taste for. Stroke after stroke he shared bits of his life. The loss of both his father and mother. The challenges of raising three children in a mountain home with no electricity or running water. The pride he has

Travels with Pa

for his children, two of whom are deaf but nevertheless made it through the 12th grade. The hour ended just as the sun was about to set.

Walking back, we stopped for dinner. Muna, the owner, said it was all fresh, then pointed to her favorite.

"I stuff it with garlic cloves, tiny mushrooms, and bits of sweet onion before putting it on the grill."

It was incredible.

While we ate I asked Pa, though I thought it unlikely, if he'd ever met Anthony Bourdain. He knew of him. Pa and Anthony share a mutual friend, a chef Pa met on his travels to Chicago. Though Pa never spoke with Mr. Bourdain, he recalled something he once said:

"No matter what it looks like, you should try every food at least once."

We arranged to meet Mr. Vishnu at the lake early the next day. We'll rent a scooter and drive into the mountains. He wants to introduce us to his family and show us around the area.

A Dear Man

March 11

We met Mr. Vishnu as planned, next to the scooter he'd secured for the day. Unlocking the tandem seat, he removed the one helmet and fitted it securely. We asked for one as well, to which Mr.

Travels with Pa

Vishnu replied, "No need to worry."

Pa had some concern, but I told him the Pokhara traffic is nothing like that of Kathmandu. And surely a man who trekked the Annapurnas for most of thirty years would transport us safely into the nearby foothills.

It was a little rough at first, a close call with a taxi unsettling. But Mr. Vishnu assured us it was the other gentleman's fault. Promising, nevertheless, that he'd exercise greater caution as we proceeded. Soon we were making the climb, a series of hairpin curves offering excellent views of the valley below. A few times, without prompting from Pa, I suggested we slow down for the oncoming traffic. Mr. Vishnu assured us, "I will go slower." There being no value in recounting the remainder of the journey, suffice it to say we arrived safely in Kaskikot, the village of Mr. Vishnu's birth. A lovely place and off the radar of the casual tourist, Mr. Vishnu suggested we relax before beginning the climb.

A revered landmark in Kaskikot is "the tree," reputed by village elders to be 2,000 years old. Mr. Vishnu had no reason to doubt their veracity, but Pa was skeptical. No matter its age, it's an impressive tree.

Next we stopped at a little place well known to Mr. Vishnu. The proprietor is a good friend and his wife, without question, makes the best coffee around. In no particular hurry, though the cool of the morning was escaping us, we purchased a bottle of water and loaf of bread then paid our bill. Walking the short distance to the trail's beginning, Pa and I assumed it would be a dirt path. Nothing of the kind. The walkway up was of stone, constructed with meticulous precision over decades.

"My father and grandfather often labored on it at the end of each trekking season."

We stopped at a small temple where Mr. Vishnu uttered the obligatory prayer, and at the home of a niece, her son nearby. We passed the dwelling of a good friend, and a cluster of houses where relatives live. As noon approached, our pace slowed, village and valley growing distant. Finally arriving at our destination, Mr. Vishnu was greeted by his very good friend, the keeper of the Kalika Temple. Before proceeding, it was required that the morning sutra be read. At its conclusion we removed our shoes and followed the keeper to the upper level, Annapurna not far off.

The bell was struck signaling entry into the first of two rooms, no photos allowed. Only the keeper could enter the inner room where the Hindu goddess Kali lives and the eternal flame is tended. Once outside, the blessing of Kali was bestowed upon Mr. Vishnu, then Pa and me. In our mind's eye, we imagined her present. Before descending, Mr. Vishnu identified from left to right the mountains of the Annapurna range then insisted a photo be taken to document our visit.

Not far from the Kalika Temple is a smaller temple rarely visited. Sharing bread and water, Mr. Vishnu explained that the faithful believe Kali to be the ultimate manifestation of Shakti, the primordial cosmic energy.

"She's the divine protector who bestows moksha: self-realization and self-knowledge. Many pilgrims visit from India, Pakistan and throughout Nepal to receive her blessing. The same blessing you received from Kali."

Mr. Vishnu, courageous man of the Annapurnas, then lowered his voice:

"Mr. Frederick, I must tell you how very sorry I am. This morning my heart was pounding. I was afraid. It was the first time I had a tall man on the back of a scooter. It was difficult. I hope you will forgive me."

How could we not, and we told him so. But then we made a suggestion:

"A few miles before arriving at Kaskikot there was the mountain end of the Annapurna cable car. Perhaps it would be best if we returned that way. Would you mind?"

Mr. Vishnu smiled his wonderful smile, "A wise suggestion Mr. Frederick."

Descending, often difficult as the going up, Mr. Vishnu at times gently took my hand.

Back in Kaskikot, we visited the home where Mr. Vishnu was born, vacant since his father's death. He hopes to restore it someday and live there in his old age with his wife.

Again on the scooter, it was a slow and easy ride to Sarangkot and the cable car. Once there, we exchanged hugs and talked briefly about dinner with his family. It may happen, but if not, we will never forget Mr. Vishnu, a very dear man.

The give and the take,
the easy in and out

Travels with Pa

the casual exchange,
the this for that,
our easy speech.
But inwardly I said,
What has made me
will be given back,
what I have loved
was loved because it was not me,
but changed me,
even as it left me,
and you who leave me now
show mercy in your going
by stirring the memory
of your first arrival ...

   -David Whyte, *Pilgrim*

Lessons From Pokhara

March 12

And some might ask,

"What can one learn in four days?"

Of resilience and survival - on the street, every day - selling a single ear of corn at a time.

Of fresh air and fellowship.

Of the necessity of child's play, always and everywhere.

Of mother's love - intimate and transcendent.

Of youthful dreams - Rohit hoping to study in America.

Of graciousness - Prabin, serving masala tea each morning at the Mountain Villa.

Of newfound friendship.

Of Ujjwal, sharing his life story and passion for service.

Of hospitality - Ujjwal and Sushma, sharing food and drink of the Nepali kind.

Of guidance, from a little man with a big heart - keeper of goats, head of family, grandparent of a new arrival.

Of the transience of evening light.

And of eternity - the great mountain looking down on all that is and ever was,

only the stones remaining of those who worshipped Kali.

Green Chwadi

March 13

Our first evening at Chwadi Green. Only the sounds of birds disturbed the silence.

We arrived in the afternoon from Pokhara aboard Buddha Air 641. Ten minutes at cruising altitude before our initial descent.

I'd not been on a twin engine prop since 1976, on a flight from Mérida, Yucatán to the ruins of Tikal. There's a certain excitement in not knowing the outcome.

Of the many possibilities at the Bharatpur airport, we chose Suresh to drive us the 40 km to Chwadi. It was a bumpy hour and a half ride, brief stretches of asphalt interrupting endless gravel and rock that took its toll on more than one vehicle.

Arriving in the heat of the afternoon at this paradise near the bank of the river, beyond which is the Chitwan National Park, we showered and rested, then sat.

"There will be stories here," Pa said. "Stories unlike any we've ever heard."

As the sun approached the end of its day, we walked the fields and passed a young woman in the water where bathing and laundry take place.

At the break of dawn, the birds announcing the new day.

Breakfast at 8, then …

Just Across the River

March 14

Up the river one kilometer from Green Chwadi is a bridge. Cross over and within a few hundred yards, you're at the entrance to a vast protected land. Home to all but a few of Nepal's Great One-Horned Rhinos, the jungle sanctuary is the pride of the Nepalese just as much as the Annapurna. And on an afternoon that would reach 90 degrees, Pa and I had the good fortune to be in the company of Sandeep Mahato, Bishal Mahato, and Jit Bahadur.

Each an accomplished guide from the Tharu community, they are expert in the ways of the Rhino, its movements, feeding habits, protective nature, and temperament, which can make it quite dangerous in certain situations and at predictable times.

We set off with Jit in the lead, followed by Sandeep, the principal spokesman, and Bishal protecting our rear. Once we arrived at the first watering hole, Sandeep informed us that "we're in their neighborhood." Shortly after, we were in the thick of it, Jit gesturing that we walk very quietly.

There's a reason Pa and I were told why Jit takes the lead: he has the keenest eye of the three and is almost always the first to see one.

No sooner had we slowed down than Jit spotted her, on the far bank of the river, young one in tow. Sandeep whispered that the female is pregnant for about 18 months, after which only a single calf is born. Weighing as much as a hundred pounds, it's up and walking within minutes. He estimated this one to be about eight weeks old.

Quite a sight, those two. We observed them for several minutes before they were prompted to move toward greater safety.

"They may have picked up our scent," Sandeep told us. "Their sight is poor, but their hearing and sense of smell is amazing."

Moving on, Bishal said we were very fortunate, as oftentimes you can walk the jungle for half a day without a single sighting.

An hour passed, and we came upon a tower.

"It's for observation, and for safety," Sandeep explained. "There are times when we must be out of their reach."

Just then, Bishal spotted another, feeding in tall grass not far away. Abruptly, the sound of an engine, perhaps a motorcycle, disturbed the silence.

"We must get to the tower," urged Jit. "Two males are fighting."

Once out of harm's way, Sandeep explained that the rhino is most dangerous during mating season and when two adult males confront each other.

"They can cover a tremendous distance in little time when they're angry."

It was peaceful at the top, the river moving lazily downstream, the grassland beyond. After several minutes, Bishal descended and beckoned for us to follow. A mother and calf were having a late lunch. They would be the last we'd see, but the afternoon wasn't over.

There were spotted deer, too quick to photograph. And monkeys sunbathing on the far shore. On the jungle floor, the scat of sloth and rhino, delicate flowers, and the footprints of rhino, wild peacock, and the Royal Bengal Tiger.

The afternoon waning, we began to make our way back, but not before one last sighting: wild boar in the distance.

Back to the forest that surrounds the jungle, we walked on gifts offered by the great trees overhead. The sun's day nearly at an end, dinner awaited at Green Chwadi.

Taking Notice

March 15

Pa and I were trained to lawyer, a useful skill at times, but a narrow way of being in the world when all is said and done.

I sometimes tell people I'm a "recovering lawyer," twelve years since formal retirement and not fully free of it. There are long stretches when the law seems eons past, but then some provocation or slight triggers a "lawyerly response," and relapse occurs.

Pa and I have talked about this. He understands. Seventy years since his own retirement, nearly sixty since Bea's passing and fifty since his own, and yet it happens, most often when he's out with friends. A simple conversation turns scholarly debate, then argument. Far removed from the courtroom, yet the urge to win rises up.

"In the moment," he told me recently, "I'm overcome by it. Later I regret it."

So when the opportunity was presented to return to the jungle with a naturalist, we seized upon it. A naturalist's way of being in the world is so foreign from ours. There's no winning or losing, or even right or wrong. A naturalist, when true to his or her calling, is in it for the *awe*, for the sheer delight of taking notice of what has always been.

We could hardly sleep. Sunrise couldn't come soon enough. And

Travels with Pa

when it did, we were already there. It's not difficult to move from Green Chwadi into the jungle, already surrounded by it, the short walk just a necessary stretch.

Suhdan was our guide, mentor, and teacher. Born Hindu Brahmin and trained as a scientist, he's highly skilled and yet possessed of an intuitive sense of the mystery energizing the natural world. Moving through what looked to Pa and me as mere thicket, he would gently command:

"Look. Look here," or "Please, listen."

At the rhino's watering hole, he pointed out the fern growing from the dung. And as the smallest of birds moved from tree to tree, he would name it, then identify it with image so it might impress upon our memories. Passing by an insignificant bush, he would call us back to see it, touch it, learn its medicinal value.

For Suhdan, the spider's dwelling is a miracle, a tree home a marvel to behold, a squirrel's tail a delight to caress. There is no hierarchy in the bird kingdom for Suhdan, the vulture no more or less important than the wild chicken, the rhino no greater than the flowers that populate the jungle floor.

Standing in the middle of grassland, he mimicked the call of nearby lovers, and then, to again impress upon our memories, searched for their image. Leading us back, he spotted something at rest, cautioned that we observe in silence, then requested we follow him on a safer path.

On our return, we came upon the familiar, respected by Suhdan just as much as the wild, and were soon back home at Green Chwadi.

The Neighborhood

March 16

What makes Green Chwadi unique, perhaps in all of Nepal, is the extent to which it embraces the indigenous communities around it, and the embrace by those communities of Green Chwadi. Bordered on the east by river and jungle, on all other sides Green Chwadi is touched by Tharu and Bote, and other indigenous communities as well.

The government says about 35 percent of the country's population is comprised of indigenous peoples. Researchers contend it's as high as 50 percent. Whatever the number, Nepal has well over 100 ethnic groups and castes, and about as many languages, all living in one of three geographic areas, the mountains, the hills, and the plains.

Since leaving Kathmandu, Pa and I have had conversations with some who know something about the character of the country's indigenous. Our takeaway is that, nearly always, they not only co-exist but do so in harmony. The lives of Green Chwadi's neighbors are by no means easy, but there's an ease in their way of being in the world that's palpable, and that few Westerners experience.

Knowing little else about the matter, we've been content to just walk through the nearest village, and let it soak in.

Travels with Pa

A Vision

March 17

We're back in Kathmandu, in the comfort of Swagat Homestay and the good company of Sugat, Roshani, and the children. It will be a while, though, before Pa and I will have truly left Green Chwadi. How will we ever forget the wise man of the Bote? So few words but a gentle spirit that says much.

I asked Pa if he remembers when I was 10 and he was nearly 90. I'd sit next to him, neither one of us saying a word. It's that same feeling. One need not be canonized to be a saint. But you must have let go of nearly everything. I believe it's that way with the wise man of Bote.

We had dinner last night at the Jacaranda, the restaurant Sugat owns with his good friend Raghav from Green Chwadi. Raghav's father met us there. The Honorable Mihir Thakur is a lawyer, former law school professor, judge, consultant, author, and now one of five members of Nepal's Human Rights Commission. Not nearly as old as the man from Bote, but the day will come when children, grandchildren and others will just want to sit by him.

We talked about Nepal's troubled history, the end of the monarchy, the insurrectionists, kidnappings, murders, the ongoing struggle to create a fair and just society, and the need for healing. As the evening moved on, we talked about family. His wife, a lawyer and long-standing member of Parliament, and his son the scientist, now teaching in Germany. We talked about Raghav, the second son of whom he is equally proud who stayed home because Nepal desperately needs him and others like him. Also trained as a lawyer with degrees in conflict studies and business as well, Raghav worked in the larger world for a while, with UNICEF and other organizations. But he had a vision, to take the best of what he'd learned to a village area of Nepal.

Disdaining profit for profit's sake, his vision was informed by others around the world engaged in social entrepreneurship, the application of business principles to social causes. In 2019, after years of discernment, he partnered with his best friend, Susan Shrestha, to embark on the "Green Chwadi Experiment." The two wanted to create a model where guests would come to rejuvenate body and soul, and at the same time support the ongoing protection and conservation of the nearby jungle and indigenous peoples.

Our third morning at Green Chwadi, Pa and I, already under the spell of the vision, did a walkabout of the center of the experiment. The women's center, under construction but nearly completed, where Tharu and Bote will engage in and teach crafts, provide hospitality on the floor above, and earn much-needed income. The new kitchen, in operation within a month, where meals will be prepared and guests will have the opportunity to enhance their skills and add to their collections of favorite recipes. The meeting house where meals are taken, music is played and dances performed. The grounds where present and future guests walk in silence or in quiet conversation. The cottages, with clean sheets and hot showers. The nearby fields where new ground is broken, crops are grown and birds nest. The natural spring providing drinking water for everyone, guests and villagers alike, and where downstream laundry is done. The Montessori school, opening in April, with a capacity of 100, 42 already enrolled.

More could be written about the Green Chwadi Experiment, but for now it will suffice to witness the manifestation of a vision and, perhaps, be motivated by it.

"Some men see things as they are, and ask why. I dream of things that never were, and ask why not." , Robert F. Kennedy

Pashupatinath

March 18

Luisa, a young German woman, arrived at Swagat the evening Pa and I returned from Green Chwadi. A naturopath by training, she'd come to Nepal for a six-week trek, after which she'll begin her career. With two days before Luisa's departure, Sugat suggested the two of us visit Pashupatinath, the most revered Hindu temple in Nepal and an easy walk from Swagat.

Setting out after breakfast, it wasn't long before Pa, Luisa, and I left the main artery and entered the narrow street leading to the temple complex. The street opened up and we fell in line with others, many of whom had traveled a great distance to pay their respects to the god Shiva. Within minutes, we were looking down on the sacred river Bagmati, smoke rising from cremation sites lining the river's bank. We spoke with Parmatma, a young man knowledgeable about the site and the practice taking place. A registered guide, we hired him to accompany us.

There is much to see at Pashupatinath. Small altars with intricate carvings. Families honoring loved ones on the anniversary of their death. Structures of reverence, one leading to another, then another, and the main Temple only Hindus can approach. Of course there are wise men revealing great truths, and monkeys wondering what life is all about, or perhaps they already know.

Arriving at the far bank of the Bagmati, Parmatma informed us that those who die at Pashupatinath are reborn as human, regardless of any misconduct during their prior lives. Pointing to a large white building across the river, "That's the Hospice. In previous times a gifted man would feel the pulse of the dying, then inform loved ones of the time remaining."

Parmatma drew our attention to a deceased being washed, then dressed for the journey. Soon after, relatives carried the body to a waiting platform where it was placed in anticipation of cremation. A few minutes later, the final process had begun. As the smoke rose, Parmatma explained that when only ashes remain they are placed in the Bagmati, which later meets the holy river Ganges.

As we observed, I shared that a few years before I'd written a novel about the American poet Walt Whitman. The novel begins when he's on his deathbed. In a dream, Whitman is informed that he's been given another year to live, provided the year begin in 21st-century America at the time of Donald Trump. Late in the book, Whitman is assigned a guide, the Egyptian goddess Isis, who takes him to death scenes around the world. One of those is at the banks of a sacred river.

As I told the story, a gentleman tapped me on the shoulder, introducing himself as Sajjad from Bangladesh. He'd overheard our conversation and wanted to know more about the book as he's a fan of Walt Whitman's. We talked for a while and learned that we share a fondness for other poets as well. In addition, a friend of his attended the University of Iowa and his sister lives in Chicago. He then shared that six months ago he'd traveled to Pashupatinath intending to commit suicide. He received emergency care just in time.

"I've returned to Pashupatinath to remind myself of how precious life is."

This morning, Pa and I reflected on our visit to Pashupatinath. I then read to him the account of Walt's visit to the river:

We continued our journey at sunrise, following the trail from the day before. By noon, what had been a pleasant stream had grown to a wide, lazy river. No longer were we on the plains. The open grassland had given way to a dark forest. From time to time there were clearings. Villages sprung up, their inhabitants supported by crops from the adjacent fields. Pressing on, the villages grew larger and more numerous. The trail widened into a path and then a road. Increasingly we shared it with other travelers, on foot, riding in carts pulled by oxen, even atop massive elephants that owned the right-of-way when coming through. Frequently a beggar would approach, rewarded by Isis with a coin from a small purse that was seemingly bottomless. The river, too, had become a highway. Long, open crafts ferried passengers from one side to the other. Occasionally a larger, more ornate vessel floated by, carrying royal travelers to unknown destinations. With sunset came light from open cooking pits and small dwellings. On the bank of the river, however, fire was used for another purpose. There were pads, eight to ten feet square, constructed of numerous flat stones. Upon them were wood supports. Funeral pyres, I soon discovered. We passed a few as yet unoccupied. But it wasn't long before we saw a large crowd gathered around one, flames licking it from its base to its highest timber and beyond. At the top was a body, wrapped in white cloth but nearly consumed by flames. Most observers were in deep mourning. As the fire died down, we could see that the flesh was no longer, leaving only charred, skeletal remains. Late in the night, when the bones had cooled but were still burning, a priestly figure pierced the skull with a bamboo poker, creating a hole to allow the release of the spirit. Soon, the pyre was reduced to embers. We reclined on the ground nearby, warmed by the remains as sleep overtook us.

The Streets of Kathmandu

March 19

Pa and I were invited to the Jacaranda for mid-afternoon momos and beer. Marco, our friend from Germany, would be there. His friend Sebastian, just arrived from Germany for a ten-day trek, would be there as well. Sugat too, and others for sure. You never know who will be at the Jacaranda.

It being a sunny afternoon, Pa and I chose to walk the 4 km, leaving Swagat Homestay with more than enough time to arrive by two, or so we thought. But once you're on the streets of Kathmandu, time takes a holiday and the feast begins. So we left at one, fifty minutes sufficient time according to Google Maps, and the journey to Jacaranda began.

To describe Kathmandu without images is a near impossibility.

Take the words required for a single fruit stand and two passers-by, multiply them by a thousand, and perhaps you would have a good start. Time and space not permitting such an endeavor, a quick stop to www.travelswithpa.com should suffice.

Momos – An Introduction

March 20

Today we learned how to make momos, a steamed dumpling, sometimes deep-fried. Momos are everywhere in Nepal. Some foods you learn to like. Momos you love from the first bite. Sugat told us more than once that he'll go to a restaurant, scan the menu for something different, and then order momos.

We gathered in the common area of Swagat Homestay, where Sugat described the momo and its history, Marco offered a visitor's perspective, and Roshani introduced us to the process.

First, there is the *keema*, the minced filling. It can be chicken, beef, pork, or buffalo, greatly favored in Nepal.

The basic ingredients are:
- Meat
- Spring onion
- Cabbage
- Radish (if you like)
- Salt
- Cumin

- Black pepper
- Ginger-garlic paste
- Pickle *(I'm still confused about "pickle." I don't think they mean what we mean by pickle.)*
- Water – just enough to moisten the mixture

Before adding the water, everything should be finely mixed, after which a simple dough is made. For every cup of keema, two cups of flour should be used., which is kneaded just like a pie crust. Small pieces are broken off, rolled into balls, flattened, and placed on a flat surface, then rolled thin, but not too thin.

Marco made a fine German effort. I struggled a bit.

Once sufficient pastries have been made - you can never make enough - they're filled with keema and the pinching begins, until you have a small, tightly enclosed dumpling. After steaming for ten minutes, it's time to eat.

They are quite amazing. Sugat says he can eat 30 or 40 in one sitting. They even passed the German test.

By the way, the basic momo sauce includes:

- Tomato
- Beans
- Coriander
- Garlic
- Cheese

Thin Places

March 21

Pa and I had been encouraged by many to visit Bhaktapur. Known as *Khwopa* by the Newari, it's the cultural capital of Nepal and dates back to the 8th century. From the 12th to the 15th centuries, it was Nepal's political capital as well, although Nepal didn't actually exist as a unified country back then. Nepal has a long and fascinating political history. Suffice it to say that for many years, Bhaktapur and the surrounding area was its own sovereign country.

Arriving at noon at the gates of the city, we paid the admission fee and were immediately approached by Santosh Thapa, a congenial man hopeful that we would secure his services as a guide. Neither Pa nor I were up to that, and explained that we preferred to explore for a while at our own pace. Concerned we might find someone else, he assured us that with twenty-five years of experience, we'd find no one better. So we struck a deal: we'd hire no one else the rest of the day and would meet him in the morning at 9:30 sharp. Shaking on it, we parted company and moved on.

We had a room for the night at Hotel Rupakot, $13, with a full breakfast. Following a short nap, we went up to the rooftop and surveyed the ancient city. It was enough to get us out the door and onto the street.

At first, we did the usual thing, looking for people engaged in the stuff of daily life. There was plenty to hold our attention:

Women visiting.

Travels with Pa

Men playing games.

Or just walking along.

But a shift occurred, as sometimes happens, and we were on the lookout for *Thin Places*. As one writer put it, "Thin places are those places where the walls are weak", like the Donegal Cliffs, or the Blue Mosque, or even some out-of-the-way tavern frequented only by locals.

Pa and I had been there, like when a stairway calls you up, or down for that matter, and you're in another place.

It may be an obscure opening, or a view that leads to a view.

It might be what appears at first to be an abandoned courtyard, yet something whispers that there's more.

An old well might beckon, and you wonder how many buckets have drawn water over the centuries.

Sometimes there are Thin Places that are inhabited, and it's difficult to tell which came first.

Or a pile of rubble juxtaposed with a bouquet of flowers draws you in, inviting you to explore the surrounding structures.

Abandoned places are particularly ripe for Thin Places so small, you must be right on top of them.

Pa and I ended our exploration with a cup of masala tea and a view of the city. In the morning, we'll do a walkabout with Mr. Thapa, knowing full well that a Thin Place or two will present itself.

Travels with Pa

Lama Sirs

March 22

A few days after Pa and I arrived, I asked Roshani if there was a school nearby, an obvious question as every morning at breakfast there were sounds of children laughing, as if just on the other side of the wall.

"That's Trevini. It's right there," she said, pointing to the building next door. "Lama Sir is the principal. He's a wonderful man."

I asked if Pa and I might meet him.

"Of course. I'll call him today."

The next morning we were seated in his office, where he told us about the children under his care. There are local students, and many from impoverished villages in the remote regions of Nepal. Of the nearly 200 students, 60 are from afar. Many are orphans. All 60 live in a large house adjacent to the school. Lama Sir lives with them as well.

I asked how he came to be principal.

Wangden Lama at birth, he was raised by middle-class parents in Darjeeling and taught by Canadian Jesuits. Having attended a Jesuit university myself, we connected. Lama Sir, that's what his students call him, left India not long after completing his university education. His sister was in Kathmandu, having started the Trevini School. He soon joined her.

Our conversation was cut short, as Lama Sir had to teach a class. But before leaving, he insisted we return in the evening to meet

Travels with Pa

some of the students.

It was an incredible three hours - listening to and learning about the circumstances of their early lives, and their recognition that education is the only way forward. At one point, Lama Sir went to his shelf to show us an example of the work the students are capable of.

Pa and I were sad the evening had to end, but the students needed to study before lights out at ten.

Yesterday, Lama Sir invited us back for the evening meal. After a tour of the kitchen and dining area, we peeked into the study area before sitting down for dinner with Lama Sir I and Lama Sir II. That's what I call them.

Lama Sir II is also from Darjeeling and Jesuit-educated. He moved to Kathmandu years ago to accept a teaching position. Last year, he resigned to work at Trevini for no pay, and to live with the students and Lama Sir I. By the way, the meal may have been the best Pa and I have had since arriving in Nepal.

This morning we returned to the school to teach Lama Sir I's first-period class. Just inside the front gate was a beautiful mural, and on the adjacent wall notices of interest for students and parents. Next to them a celebration of Women's Day.

The school courtyard was quiet, as Pa and I were a few minutes late. We peeked into a classroom, where Science was being taught to third-level students, and then found Lama Sir I taking attendance. For the next hour, Pa and I had the privilege of conversing with these remarkable students about what they want their lives to look like.

On the way out, no time to talk with Lama Sir I as he had another class, a young one gave us a hug. It made our day.

Faces of Nepal

March 23

Pa and I spent the evening looking at photos. As beautiful as Nepal is, time and again we returned to the faces. So many are compelling and will forever be unforgettable. They are faces to be spread around, shared, alerting those who've yet to travel to Nepal that it's not too late.

There is a place in the world where kindness is a genetic trait.

I recall reading a book by a Jesuit scholar who contended that each country, or at least each region, has a particular genius. The Germans for precision and orderliness. The Italians for art and architecture. The French for cooking, perhaps. And so on.

The Nepalese, I believe, have a genius for connecting, for reaching out to strangers. It may not be universal. There are exceptions, and the circumstances of life can make it difficult. But Pa and I experienced enough kindness to know that in Nepal, it's the norm, not the anomaly.

Take a minute, if you have time, to visit www.travelswithpa.com where we share many of the faces we met along the way, and will never forget.

CHAPTER SEVEN
Malaysia

Lady Of The Night

March 24

We never intended to stay long in Kuala Lumpur. It's a big city - sleek and modern. Not Dubai by any means, but not where we wanted to be. So after a morning in the park near the Petronas Towers, we flew north an hour to Penang International and taxied to George Town. Arriving mid-afternoon, it was oppressively hot. And not just in George Town. Bangkok, 95. Ho Chi Minh City the same. We'll be sweating our way through SE Asia. My son-in-law Zac said when he and Sarah honeymooned in these parts, he never stopped.

"I was legitimately concerned that Sarah would get an annulment for irreconcilable perspiration the moment we got home."

So after arriving, Pa and I stayed in the cool of our room, missing Nepal and feeling sorry for ourselves. Actually it was just me. Pa didn't think the heat would bother him one bit, and come dinner time he pushed us out the door.

The sun about to set, we were in some strange kind of Wonderland, and would like to have had Alice along. Rounding a corner the Call to Prayer sounded, a reminder that more than half of Malaysia's population is Muslim. We were in an old part of the city for sure, but not just old. When the lamplights awakened, we knew, this is a town of Thin Places.

Every corner, every street, every step of the way. I felt a little guilty. Though my heart was still in Nepal, I was being seduced by a lady of the night. Pa blushed at the thought of it and said we best be getting dinner. Soon enough, on a back street of George Town, what everyone comes to SE Asia for. I told the gentleman it was late and couldn't eat much. I don't think he understood. We made our way through most of it just as the Call to Prayer sounded, and happened to look to the left.

Settling up, we went there, and were reminded that it's Ramadan. Not wanting to intrude, we resumed our walk with the lady of the night, a most fascinating woman to say the least. Somehow we were back on the street that started it all, and soon home, in the comfort of Carnarvon House.

In Search of Anthony

March 25

We'd read about George Town's incredible food. For its size, it's reputed to rival Bangkok, Saigon, Hanoi - hose legendary cities where people eat on the streets. As breakfast isn't served at Carnarvon House, Pa suggested we take our time and see what lunch might bring.

"There's a chance we'll run into Anthony Bourdain," he said. "If the street food is as good as they say, this is his kind of town."

Travels with Pa

Having visited once with Anthony, Pa knows a thing or two about street food. They have a mutual acquaintance, a chef in Chicago whose restaurant Pa used to frequent. He learned from Anthony that you look for places where people are standing, waiting to get in. Places where you can see what you're getting and watch it being made.

"If we bump into Anthony, we'll know we're at the right place."

We saw many possibilities, but no Anthony. On a side street, though, something caught our eye: a mother and daughter preparing what we later learned was *Nombu Kanji*. Siti, the daughter, told us it's an Indian porridge served every evening during Ramadan.

"My mom and I are here every morning making it for the restaurant around the corner."

Sakina, the mother, showed us what goes into it and some of the preparation.

"Always you have coconut milk and moong dal," she explained. "Then tomato, carrot, curry, chili, and many other spices. Then you cook it and cook it, and this is what you have," she said with a smile.

"You come back in an hour. We'll feed you."

We assured Sakina we'd be back, Anthony or not.

An hour to spare, we went looking for a tailor to turn my pants into shorts, the heat being what it is. Along the way, there was one Thin Place after another. One we would have liked to enter, but couldn't. If Alice had been with us, perhaps we could have.

Travels with Pa

Time got away from us, and we returned late. But Siti greeted us with soup in a bag, which we'll have for dinner.

We resumed our search, for Anthony and for lunch, and happened upon Jin's Place, where we could see the food and how it was prepared. No Anthony, but we're certain he would have enjoyed it.

Pa Takes a Holiday

March 26

I fly to Bangkok today. Without Pa. He says Bea is missing him, and that it's spring training. Truth is, I think he's homesick. Since passing more than seventy years ago, it's the first time Pa's been away from Bea.

Not wanting to provoke, I asked Pa about spring training, knowing that after he retired, he'd spent time with the Cardinals in Florida. I assumed that's what he was alluding to. But he surprised me.

"You know my dad was a coal miner. We had little when I was a boy. When you're poor, people tend to look down on you. Sports was my way of leveling the playing field."

It all made sense then, the photos of Pa. Captain of his high school baseball team. And of his football team.

I asked how long he'd be away.

"A week or two. Long enough to catch up with Bea and get

together with my teammates. We'll play a few games. It'll be just like old times."

Concerned he might injure himself, I suggested he take it easy.

"No need to worry, young man. Where I come from, you can be whoever you were in your previous life. Every spring, I'm captain of the team."

It being Pa's last day for a while, I asked what he'd like to see.

"The Blue Mansion, of course. I've heard so much about it. Built by Cheong Fatt Tze in the 19th century, 38 rooms, five courtyards, seven staircases, and 220 windows."

I asked how he knew such things.

"I know Cheong. Nice fellow. Born poor like me. Later he became Consul-General of China, director of China's largest bank, and helped build the country's first railway. I can identify. He built the Blue Mansion as a testament to his life's work. I did the same for Bea, having promised her years before that I would."

It was an easy walk from Carnarvon House. But when we arrived, a sign said it was closed to the public. We peered through the barrier. There were cars. We approached the gate. The guard said we couldn't enter.

I told Pa we could go elsewhere. He'd have none of it. He knew the pain of exclusion. So I suggested we make the most of it and see what we could see.

We looked up and admired the detail. Caught glimpses of the blue as best we could. And there were the flowers, free to be seen by anyone. On the walk back, we talked about what it's like to

Travels with Pa

be on the outside looking in.

"It gives you a certain perspective," Pa said. "One the privileged often lack. How many who drive through that gate stop to appreciate the art, or smell the flowers given to us freely?"

I knew Pa was right. But we'd seen so many who are excluded, who never even get close to the gate. I wondered about them but didn't want to disturb Pa with my thoughts.

That evening, we strolled through one of the Clan Jetties. Chinese immigrants built homes on those jetties about the time the Blue Mansion was built. There are no barriers on the jetties, and the view is far superior.

I woke this morning with an ache. Pa had left. But I knew he'd be back. The Dutch always follow through.

CHAPTER EIGHT
Thailand

Pa Checks In

April 1

Pa checked in. I had a feeling he would. He'd never admit it, but he doesn't like being left out any more than anyone else. In some respects, Pa is still human.

It was earlier evening as I was walking over a bamboo bridge in the hills north of Pai. Skirting the forest edge, I approached a Buddhist temple.

"Young man. It's been a while. How are you doing?"

I didn't want to say it had only been a few days and I was doing just fine. Instead, I told him I'd been missing him.

"I thought that might be the case," he said. "That's why I stopped by."

I asked about his time away.

"It's been good. Bea and I have had a chance to catch up. I've visited with my parents and grandparents too, and played a lot of baseball. I don't think I told you, our games last at least a hundred innings and always end in a tie. There are no winners or losers here. I still love hitting home runs though."

Then Pa asked about my time.

Travels with Pa

"It's been good," I told him. "Jen was in Bangkok the day I arrived. That evening we took a river cruise, and the next morning I had a three-hour massage. After lunch we flew to Chiang Mai, and the next morning took a van to Pai, three hours and 175 hairpin turns."

I told him Pai is a mountain town with a lot of young people who come for the hiking and rafting, the food and drink, and the marijuana. It reminds me of the old days. Of course, I didn't tell Pa that.

He started talking about the Buddha.

"He's well respected here. Always has a good audience and is never preachy. Just wants people to relax. It takes some a long time to get ambition and anxiety out of their systems. I struggled with that at the beginning. Baseball, the way we play it, has helped a lot. Along with meditation every seven innings."

I told Pa the Buddha has quite a following in Thailand too, and showed him a few photos.

"I'll make sure to tell him," Pa said, as his voice faded with the setting sun.

We Can Only Hope

April 4

I don't recall when I became certain there was no other way out. But for years now, I've believed that the only chance our planet has for survival is if women are in charge. To be honest, the male of the species has had its chance, and failed. Men still have a role, to be sure, but that's another conversation.

Lately, I've been thinking about Caitlin Clark, leading her team to the national championship game. How could I not? The best player in women's basketball, playing for my home state Iowa Hawkeyes. Juliann was an all-state center at the same high school Caitlin attended. I went there too, fifty years earlier. But it's not just the local connection. Caitlin is a force, skilled, passionate, and inspiring, encouraging those around her, girls and boys alike, to be their best.

I've also been thinking about my girls.

Kate, trained as a social worker, is now a manager for a large electrical contractor. Her strength is lifting others up, she'll be president of the company someday, I'm sure.

Juliann, once a leader on the court, now oversees maternal and child health programs for the state of Iowa.

Sarah, a psychiatrist, works with children and adolescents who've suffered trauma.

Mary, our dog whisperer, is a nurse and now deep into doctoral studies, committed to equal access in mental health care.

And Julia, Phil's wife, a psychologist who tends the hidden compassionate instincts in medical students, teaching them the quiet, unquantifiable art of healing.

I've added a new hero to my list: Sangduen "Lek" Chailert.

Honored as one of six Global Conservation Females and named a "Hero of Asia" by *Time* magazine, she was recently awarded

Travels with Pa

France's *Légion d'Honneur* by President Macron for her work protecting elephants and the environment.

Born in a mountain village in northern Thailand, Lek was raised by her grandfather, a village shaman who treated the sick and injured, both human and animal. She learned much from him. In her early twenties, she rescued her first elephant. Over the next decade, others followed, one by one, until she established the Elephant Nature Park north of Chiang Mai in 2003.

Jen and I spent most of a day at the sanctuary. Today, 114 elephants roam freely, mother and child, young and old, each tended by a trained, compassionate caregiver. Many were rescued from illegal logging operations, blinded by the cruel hooks used to control them. Others were broken by trekking companies, serving tourists who'd rather ride than walk. Some came from circuses, torn from their mothers and left traumatized for life. Some were victims of poachers.

Lek is not alone in her mission, others in India, Africa, and Southeast Asia are doing similar work, but she is in it for the long haul. The sanctuary is a testament to her tenacity.

And interestingly, even in elephant society, the pattern holds: males go off alone after adolescence, while females stay, committed for life to the family.

After receiving the *Légion d'Honneur*, Lek made a promise:

To the end of my life, I will stand up and work to safeguard our natural resources, and to be a voice for the silent creatures who enrich this web of Life called Home.

There are women like Lek at nearly every level of modern life, quietly, powerfully changing the world. We can only hope a critical mass is reached in time.

Holding the Irreconcilable

April 6

I didn't grow up going to museums, certainly not art museums. I think my first visit was in eighth grade, a field trip to the Iowa Historical Museum. It was memorable mostly because of the biplane suspended from the ceiling.

My first real exposure to art came in college through an American art history course. As part of the class, we were required to visit the St. Louis Art Museum. I was drawn to the great paintings, especially those that told a story. The more narrative, the better. I had no interest in the pottery, ceramics, jewelry, or textiles. To me, they were just artifacts, mute and static.

But late in life, and especially since leaving home, I've come to understand that the artifacts *are* the story. They reveal the arc of human progress in ways that paintings and sculptures often do not. They speak to a genius for process, developed anonymously and refined over generations.

We visited the National Museum of Thailand on our last morning in Bangkok. There were no framed paintings on the walls, no freestanding sculptures. But the sensitive, detailed art of the Thai people across centuries was stunning.

There were miniature *Khon* masks, made of papier-mâché, deco-

Travels with Pa

rated with gilded lacquer, and inlaid with gems.

A great Ganesha *Khon* mask with mother-of-pearl inlay.

A ceramic dish depicting the life of the Buddha, outlined in gold enamel.

A large, gilded lacquer painting illustrating multiple scenes from the *Ramakien*, including the abduction of Sita.

Musical instruments, exquisite and sculptural in form.

Puppets that told stories of passion and intrigue.

Panels and doors that served a purpose beyond mere opening and closing. Containers of every shape, each one purposeful and beautiful.

Near the end of the visit, a familiar feeling arose, one I often experience in museums: the quiet discomfort that much of what we admire today would not exist without the wealth and privilege that enabled its creation. That behind so many exquisite objects lies a legacy of monarchies, ruling classes, and the rich taking from the poor.

It's a notion that's troubled me for a long time. But maybe that discomfort is a Western inheritance, a mind split by opposites, by good and bad, by blame and righteousness. The Eastern mind, it seems, is more agile, more at ease holding the irreconcilable. No wonder it is a mind shaped by the *Tao Te Ching*:

The Tao doesn't take sides,

it gives birth to both good and evil.

Travels with Pa

The Master doesn't take sides,

she welcomes both saints and sinners.

And by the *Bhagavad Gita*:

I am the ritual and the worship,

the medicine and the mantra,

the butter burnt in the fire,

and I am the flames that consume it.

I am the father of the universe

and its mother, essence and goal

of all knowledge, the refiner, the sacred

Ôm, and the threefold Vedas.

I am the heat of the sun,

I hold back the rain and release it.

I am death, and the deathless,

and all that is or is not.

CHAPTER NINE
Hong Kong

Easter in Hong Kong

April 9

Easter in Hong Kong. An oxymoron, if ever there was one. This "special administrative region of China," home to nearly 8 million residents packed into 420 square miles, doesn't seem the likeliest place to celebrate a Christian feast. Here, trade and finance are king, and the city pulses with movement and efficiency. But among the crowd, 1.3 million are Christian, and over 400,000 are Catholic.

On a cool, cloudy Easter morning, I stepped out of the behemoth complex where I'm staying and set out in search of a sanctuary. The streets were busy, business as usual, Easter notwithstanding. But taking a shortcut through a narrow passage, those nearly always lead somewhere, I emerged onto a quieter thoroughfare and soon came upon Rosary Church of Hong Kong.

Assuming I'd missed the morning Mass, I peered inside anyway. To my surprise, I was the last to arrive. No one seemed to mind. I stood in the back, as many do on high feast days.

The language was Chinese, not a word of it familiar, but the liturgy, ancient and unchanging, was unmistakable. Across the world, the shape of the Mass endures. I lingered afterward, watching the reverent and the relaxed alike, parishioners chatting easily with their pastor and with one another.

But by noon, my stomach had other plans. I went in search of an Easter meal. Duck was a contender, but I ended up choosing the local soup instead. Delicious.

Hu Meichun, a sweet woman with a wide smile, served me. Curious about the soup, I asked her what it was. Using her phone's translator, different from mine, she answered:

"Fish egg river."

We both chuckled, though I'm not sure she caught the joke.

She wanted to know where I was from. "America," I told her.

"Have you ever been there?" I asked.

Her translated reply: "Never eat an American."

More chuckles.

It's not easy being away from family on Easter Sunday. With the exception of the first COVID Easter, it's never happened. But I'll be with them by FaceTime once the grandkids are up from their naps.

I'm sure Mr. Bunny will be there, too.

Walt's Reminder

April 10

My ticket from Tokyo recently purchased, I fly home in 60 days. Already, I feel the faint pangs of loss. There is a grief that arises as

Travels with Pa

one approaches the end of a long journey. I knew it in the final weeks of a year and a half spent hitchhiking. And five years later, aboard a freighter bound for Miami after six months in Central America. More recently, I grieved in the last days of my journey with Walt Whitman, knowing he would soon die and that I would never again write of his life in the 21st century.

I hope to talk with Pa about this - the end of one life and the beginning of another. What it's like to know that there will be a last day, a last breath.

There was a time I read a poem a day, every day, and that ended. But I've picked up *Leaves of Grass* again and begun anew with *Song of Myself*:

I celebrate myself,

And what I assume you shall assume,

For every atom belonging to me as good belongs to you.

I loafe and invite my soul,

I lean and loafe at my ease,

observing a spear of summer grass ...

The old man had slapped me upside the head, reminding me that it's *today* that counts, and no other.

So I'll take the cable car this morning over Tung Chung Bay, arriving at the Po Lin Monastery. Perhaps Pa will be there and we'll marvel at the great bronze Tian Tan Buddha. Maybe I'll read to him Walt's account of sitting with the faithful as the Buddha neared the end:

"Despite his grave condition, he spoke with gentle concern to his disciples.

The teachings which I have given you, I gained by following the path myself. You should follow them and conform to their spirit on every occasion.

Then, with but a moment remaining, he uttered his last words:

Make of yourself a light. Rely upon yourself. Do not depend on anyone else. Make my teachings your light.

And so, he left them to go their own way."

If Pa returns with me, I might also read from *Leaves of Grass*, where Walt reminds us of the challenge of every journey, no matter what that journey may be:

Stop this day and night with me and you shall possess the origin of all poems,

You shall possess the good of the earth and sun, there are millions of suns left,

You shall no longer take things at second or third hand,

nor look through the eyes of the dead,

nor feed on the spectres in books.

You shall not look through my eyes either, nor take things from me,

You shall listen to all sides and filter them from yourself.

I have heard what the talkers were talking, the talk of the beginning and the end,

But I do not talk of the beginning or the end.

There was never any more inception than there is now,

Nor any more youth or age than there is now,

And will never be any more perfection than there is now,

Nor any more heaven or hell than there is now.

Tai O

April 11

It can be a good thing to start the day with a plan, have it vanquished by poor timing, and be forced to begin again.

My landlady for the week stopped me on the way out.

"What you do today?"

"I'm taking the cable car to see Tian Tan Buddha."

"Not good idea."

"Why?"

"It's holiday."

"What holiday?"

"Easter."

Travels with Pa

"Easter was yesterday."

"Easter four days in Hong Kong. Start Friday. End today. Many people see Buddha today. You go to Tai O. Much quieter."

Soon enough, I was on the Metro to Central Station. From there, the underground walk to Hong Kong Station, the train to Tung Chung, and Bus 11 to Tai O, two hours from the heart of the city. It *ought* to be quiet.

On the way, I learned that Tai O, on the far western shore of Lantau Island, is the historical home of the Tanka boat people. Still a fishing village, it's also known for its lively market, drawing people from Hong Kong and beyond. It might not be quiet after all.

Stepping off the bus, I was immediately in the thick of it. Early lunch for many, a shopping hour for others. Still a fishing village, yes, but other foodstuffs were on offer, and souvenirs too. As much as I enjoy the bustle of the marketplace, I'd come for peace and quiet.

"Walk on," the voice said.

And so I did. The market faded behind me, giving way to the back streets of private lives, small altars, and hidden places of reverence. I wanted to linger, but again the voice whispered, "walk on."

And a new world appeared. A world of stilted homes and quiet canals. Fishing boats bobbing in the soft tide. This is where the Tanka people live, and where they work.

I lingered again. But the voice came, softer now. So I left the

Tanka behind and was greeted by countryside and hills rising gently above.

Not long after, I reached what I thought was the path's end, until a middle-aged couple from Hong Kong asked if I'd take their photo. Then, kindly, they asked:

"Have you been to the top?"

I hadn't. They offered directions to a trail of steps leading up, and up, and up. Eventually I arrived where sea and sky met in quiet embrace, a lookout commemorated by sculptures of the Chinese White Dolphin, rare and sacred to these waters.

As evening arrived, I descended, the path marked by ancestral burial sites.

Having walked full circle, I thought of Pa, and imagined his time away with family and friends. I thought of my landlady, too, and was grateful for the day she had planned.

Wise Ones

April 12

Standing before it, I wondered what the Buddha would think, this oversized and exaggerated likeness that surely bears little resemblance. And yet I was in awe, as much for the effort and devotion that brought it into being as for the image itself.

"I've been wondering the same thing, young man. Just so you know, having seen the Buddha up close, it looks nothing like

Travels with Pa

him."

It was Pa, of course. I thought he might show up.

"When did you arrive?" I asked.

"When you did."

"How did you get here?"

"I just did. And how did you get here?" As if he didn't know. But I showed him photos anyway.

I asked if he might stay long enough for us to look around together.

"Of course. I can think of nothing better."

It's a lovely place, high atop the hill, looking out to sea. Pa drew my attention to a pot, low to the ground.

"What do you see?"

"A beautiful flower," I said.

"Now what do you see?"

"Oh my." Taken aback by its mystery.

"How have you been?" I asked.

"That can wait. More importantly, how have you been?"

I told him about Thailand - Jen's visit, the food, gentle people.

"They're not the same here," I said. "I can't quite put my finger on it, but the energy is different. Too much, perhaps. The constant movement. Tiresome."

"Oh really," he mused. "Let's take a walk. There's a special place

Travels with Pa

not far from here. They call it the Wisdom Path. We'll get there through the woods."

We walked in silence for a while, content with the quiet.

Then Pa spoke.

"I want to tell you about a friend of mine, Chuang. Nice man. Born the same month and year as me, but in a small village halfway around the world. Funny fellow. Always makes me think. Just the other day he said:

'Fred, all men know the use of the useful, but few know the use of the useless.'

"I've been thinking about that ever since. I kind of get it now."

Then Pa told a story Chuang had shared with him.

**"You know, the Chinese are fond of rabbits. They consider them very wise. There's a myth about a rabbit born centuries ago who still lives. As a youth, he was frail and unremarkable, with little hope or joy. One day the Wise One of the Clan approached the young rabbit. The Wise One had a way about him, and the young one opened up. They talked for hours, and again the next day, and the next.

On the fourth day, the Wise One said:

'Tonight is the full moon. I want you to sit where no one can see you, but where you can see everyone. Return to me after the next full moon and tell me what you learned.'

The young rabbit did as instructed, and when he returned, he was a new rabbit, humble, grateful, wise beyond his years."

Pa finished just as we arrived at the Wisdom Path, thirty-eight wooden columns bearing the Heart Sutra in flowing calligraphy.

"You know, young man," he said, "there are Wise Ones everywhere. You need only pay attention. And not just among humans. Every species has its Wise Ones. They come in all shapes and sizes. Each unique, in accordance with their being."

We grew quiet again, then began the walk back to the cable car. Pa enjoyed the ride immensely, and when we arrived in Tung Chung, he suggested we rest in a small park near the Metro.

"That flower we looked at earlier," he said. "People are like that too. Each a mystery."

And on the return, I saw people differently, and imagined their individual lives.

Remaining Days

April 13

Pa and I spoke at breakfast. I sensed something was bothering him and asked how he was feeling.

"I'm fine, but thank you, Fred, for your concern."

It was the first time since I was a boy that Pa had addressed me by my given name.

He continued.

"Since returning, I've been thinking about the remaining days. There aren't many. When we started in January, it seemed like a long time. But now…"

"But Pa, you'll be around for eternity, won't you? Or at least until everything spirals down to the Omega Point. You know, the big dot."

"Yes, that's what they tell us. But when I speak of remaining days, I mean the time you and I have left together."

He grew quiet, then asked, "You'll keep me around until the end, won't you?"

"Of course I will."

He then wondered if I had the photos, the ones I showed him on the train to Barcelona. I did, and removed them from my wallet. Of the six, he took hold of the one from his retirement party.

"You see here, my expression? Many would say I look sad, my career having come to an end. But to the contrary. I was feeling regret, regret that I hadn't retired earlier. Had I known then what I know now, I would have left much sooner, as you did. I worked too hard, and for too long. Whatever energy I might have had to explore the world had already left me."

I felt sad for dear Pa, and took his hand.

"There's something else," he said. "We can return only once, and only if requested by someone with whom we had a special relationship. The window is so small it rarely opens among the billions of souls. To allow constant back and forth would create a rift in the universe, and no one knows the outcome of that. Not even Einstein and his brethren."

Travels with Pa

He paused, then inquired if I knew of the poet Rainer Rilke. I told him I did.

"He's a friend now. I've come to like poets more than others, even the novelists. Like Chuang and me, René was born in 1875. Just before I returned, he read this aloud. He wrote it at 28, and it stayed with him until his death at 50."

You see, I want a lot.

Maybe I want it all.

The darkness of each endless fall.

The shimmering light of each ascent.

So many are alive who don't seem to care.

Casual, easy, they move in the world

as though untouched.

But you take pleasure in the faces

of those who know they thirst.

You cherish those who grip you for survival.

You are not dead yet.

It's not too late to open your depths

by plunging into them,

Travels with Pa

and drink in the life

that reveals itself quietly there.

"Fred," Pa said softly, "I want a lot too in my remaining days. I want to know the sea and sky. Ride boats. Gaze at great buildings. Visit little shops. Be with the people. And when the end is near, I want to visit my old high school, the courthouse, the house where Bea and I and the girls lived all those years. I want to go home one last time. Can we do that?"

I promised we'd do it all, beginning today.

And so we did. We boarded an early ferry at Tsim Sha Tsui pier. On the crossing to Hong Kong Island, we gazed at towers and took delight in the passing boats. When it was time to return, we did the same.

Disembarking, we made our way to Nathan Road, passing upscale shops and older buildings, too many to count. After a time, the new gave way to the worn. We arrived at the edge of Yau Ma Tei, the former village where anything can be purchased. It's heart is the market, stretching half the length of the street and branching into the side streets as well.

Then the complexion changed, and a certain service replaced the goods. Pa and I were saddened by the sight, though not surprised. As a judge, Pa once accepted the pleas of many such women. And I, as a state's attorney, prosecuted many of their cases. Neither of us took pleasure in our roles, knowing full well that their profession was merely the manifestation of deep and long-lasting wounds.

Travels with Pa

In the evening, we turned in early, weary from two days on the move.

Reviewing photos from four days in Hong Kong, I recalled a passage from *The Art of Stillness*, Pico Iyer's slim classic:

We glimpse a stranger on the street, and the exchange lasts a moment. But we go home and think on it and try to understand what the glance meant, spinning futures and fantasies around it. An experience that lasts an instant plays out for a lifetime inside us, becoming the story of our lives.

CHAPTER TEN
Taiwan

Taiwan 101

April 14

While Walt was away, I made an executive decision. Rather than Vietnam, temperatures near 100, I'd travel to Hong Kong and then Taiwan, hoping Walt would appreciate the cooler weather. He did, saying as much on yesterday's flight. In fact, with onboard Wi-Fi, he suggested we research the once-Portuguese Formosa, now the Republic of China.

And so, just before touching down at Taipei International, we concluded our introduction to the "Little Giant" that causes Xi Jinping such angst. Granted, our research was limited, given the short flight, but we're hoping it will suffice until we get our feet on the ground.

Taiwan is a long, thin island, less than 300 miles top to bottom, midway between the East and South China Seas. It's closer to the northern tip of the Philippines than to the southern tip of Japan. Most of the population is Taiwanese, with mainland Chinese a distant second. Fortunately, some indigenous people remain, mostly in the central highlands.

Buddhists and Taoists make up the majority of those reporting a "religious" affiliation, which makes sense given Taiwan's reputation for peace and civility. The population is fairly evenly spread from birth through age 74, though more than 5% are 75 or older.

You get a lot of Taiwan dollars for just a few U.S., and if you want to call home, you generally have to do it the day before.

The Taiwan Blue Magpie is the national bird, Beef Noodle Soup the national dish, and Taiwan Beer is favored by 87% of those who imbibe.

We arrived well after dark at the Taipei Triple Tiger Inn. It was too late to explore, but we're looking forward to our first sunrise in another new land, and hope to order our first bowl of beef noodle soup.

Street Stories

April 15

Some say man is a mythmaker, and that what separates him from other primates are the stories told to make sense of the world. I don't know enough to judge the truth of it, but I do believe the world has stories to offer, time permitting.

It rained off and on until noon. We couldn't recall the last time we had a "stay-at-home morning," as Lorelai calls them.

It's okay. Pa and I had hoped to visit Maekong Village, Taiwan's tea-growing center. Perhaps tomorrow. It's not going anywhere. We did venture out in the afternoon, however, but not beyond the neighborhood.

Travels with Pa

I read an article recently about a Mumbai artist who leads locals on walking tours. They never go beyond the neighborhood. In his experience, most don't know the nearby, assuming that what's of interest always lies elsewhere. With that in mind, we set out, in search of nothing in particular.

Our street looked different from the night of our arrival. Each time of day has its place, of course. Light, shadow, and the movement of strangers hold a certain allure. But daylight is for the details. Just around the corner is a laundry, a good find. It's been a month. A few doors down is a barber, and a little restaurant. At the corner, a grocery. Across from it a general store. A short distance further: a workplace for seamstresses, a hangout for locals, and a garden in progress.

There's an intersection where the buildings are taller. One in particular caught my eye. But Pa pointed to one adjacent, suggesting it might be of greater interest. Soon after, we were at the Ching Shui Yen Tsu Shih Temple, home to the deity that protects the An-Hsi people. The altar was compelling and deserving of respect. Overhead, stories were told of a time when myth and the day-to-day were inextricable. We lamented the passing of that magical time.

On our walk back, we happened on a park, its art not as compelling as that of the temple. But Pa suggested we slow down. Stories were being told, he said. Simple and profound. Stories of feeling, of sadness, and of possible futures. Stories demanding to be heard, each told in the art of the day by young people, I presume. Angry, prophetic, and occasionally hopeful. There's little else to say, our generation having failed those who've come after.

Instead, we went searching for soup, and found a possibility. I pulled out the scrap of paper the young man had given us. The waitress nodded and soon delivered the best meal we'd had since Kathmandu.

Saturday Night Out

April 16

It had been a while, and we were ready for a night out. Jaden, the young man at the front desk, suggested we visit Liberty Square.

"There's much to see," he said, "but you must go when it's dark, and enter through the Arch. But have you had dinner?"

We hadn't, and were considering Beef Noodle Soup again.

"If you've not had Taiwanese Stone Hot Pot," he replied, "you must. Noodle Soup is for any day. Hot Pot is for a Saturday night out."

"Where do you suggest?"

"The Delectable Hot Pot Lab. It's on the way to Liberty Square. If you leave soon, it won't be busy."

Jaden drew us a quick map, and ten minutes later we were there.

Neither Pa nor I knew what to expect, but we soon learned that it's a process. After placing our order, a staff member arrived to guide us through the ritual. A hot plate, flush with the tabletop, served as our stage. The stone pot was placed on it, and the show began: onions sautéed first, then beef, then a generous pour of water to bring it all to a boil. A minute or so later, noodles and assorted vegetables were added.

We didn't know the names of some of them, so the gentleman to our left leaned in and used Google Translate on our behalf.

The sequence continued: the beef was removed, then the broth ladled out, and finally the greens and mushrooms joined the pot. Over the course of an hour, the stone cauldron yielded three rich cups of soup, something I could happily eat every week.

By the time we finished, night had fallen. We moved on, passing Taipei East Gate, then through the grand Arch and onto Liberty Square, where we stood quietly, taking it all in. As Jaden had described, the Chiang Kai-shek Memorial Hall rose to our left, the National Theater stood to our right, and the Memorial Library faced us from the far end. Ascending the Library's massive steps, we turned to see the view stretching wide across the city.

The evening turning cool, we wandered back through the park that parallels the Square, pausing at Yunhan Lake to look once more in the direction from which we'd come, a magical sight.

We took a different route home, passing a Taoist shrine, threading through Peace Park and one of many vibrant night markets, until finally we reached our landmark and our street, where others were still enjoying their own Saturday night out.

Travels with Pa

A Lesson in Oolong

April 17

In preparing for Taipei (Pa was of little help), I read an article about Maokong, a small community just north of the city. For over a century, the mountain village has been a center for tea cultivation in Taiwan. Settlers from Fujian Province brought native Tie-Guan-Yin roots with them, and before long, local tea masters discovered that the area's misty climate and hilly soil were ideal for growing prized oolong.

Maokong isn't easy to reach by public transit. But give credit where it's due, Pa found out that we could make the one-way trip by cable car in about thirty minutes. I asked if there had been any recent malfunctions. He shrugged.

"I didn't research that far."

On paper, Maokong reads like a quiet village. But on a weekend afternoon, it's anything but. So we didn't linger. With a road to the left and another to the right, we took the one less traveled and soon found ourselves in the countryside, surrounded by tea fields.

Twenty minutes in, we were beckoned along a stone path. We followed, of course. Eventually, we were invited into a modest teahouse. Accepting the invitation, we climbed a narrow staircase and found a welcoming space known far and wide as the Lin Ji Kiang Teahouse , 六季香茶坊.

A warm, affable man greeted us.

Travels with Pa

"I'm Chaomien Liu," he said. "But please, call me Liu. Everyone does."

Liu went over the tea menu and suggested 特製冷凍茶, a favored oolong.

"It has the flavor of light champagne and the aroma of orchids. Our current tea master, Zhang Xing Zhong, spent over a decade perfecting it. It's… well, it's perfect."

He reviewed the food menu too. I told him I wasn't very hungry, that a soup would suffice.

"I suggest our noodle soup with tea oil," he said. "And perhaps some dumplings?"

A cup of tea, a bowl of soup, and a couple of dumplings sounded just right.

A few minutes later, Liu returned with a tray and began setting up. He started heating water in the pot to the left.

"Watch for the tiny bubbles forming on the bottom," he instructed.

While we waited, he told us that Zhang Nai-Miao, born in 1875 (Pa approved), was the first to bring Tie-Guan-Yin bushes from Fujian in 1895.

"His great-great-grandson is now our tea master," Liu added. "And I teach the proper way of preparing and serving his oolong."

When bubbles had begun to form. Liu removed the pot and poured the water over loose leaves resting in a fine strainer.

"First pour, no more than thirty seconds."

He filled my cup with the light amber brew. As he did, he explained that fresh tea leaves must be "withered" at precise temperatures, then agitated and bruised.

"This aids fermentation," he said, "releasing enzymes that coax phenol-rich juices and preserve the original floral aroma."

I was impressed, as was Pa.

"This man knows his oolong," he whispered.

Liu pointed to a slight red blush under the damp leaves.

"That's the sign that fermentation has taken place."

I took a sip, and there it was: champagne and orchids. Liu left us to our tea, four cups over the next half hour, before returning with soup and dumplings. Somehow, we made it through it all. Pa thought the champagne helped.

An hour later, we shook Liu's hand and thanked him for the lesson, the tea, and a most gracious afternoon.

The Train to Taitung

April 18

Pa and I both had the itch, to hop a train and ride the rails to someplace new. Having only seen Taipei, we didn't know what was possible. But after all our travels together, we've learned that almost anything is.

Travels with Pa

Lacking a guidebook, we studied a map. North, east, or west wouldn't give us the journey we craved. But south, yes, south was the ticket. And a train would take us there.

Pa grew up with trains, as did I, and knowing Walt as he does, Pa recited a few lines:

The walking beam of the steam-engine, the throttle and governors, the up and down rods,

the cart of the carman, the snow plough and two engines pushing it,

the ride on the express train.

My earliest memories are with my father, a switchman on the Rock Island Line. When I was old enough, and could make it through the night without complaint, he'd take me into the yard, where I rode in the lead engine beside his engineer buddy. From the window of that great beast, I'd watch my father at work, coupling and uncoupling boxcars, cattle cars, and tankers bound for elsewhere.

Neither Pa nor I expected to recreate the experiences of our youth. But to ride the rails is always a thrill, no matter how quiet the journey may be.

If you've traveled in Southeast Asia, Hong Kong, Taiwan, or Japan, you know that 7-Elevens are everywhere, and you can buy almost anything, including train tickets. We stopped at the one closest to the Taipei Triple Tiger, and with the help of a young clerk, had tickets in hand within minutes. The next afternoon, we'd board the 426 at Banqiao Station - destination Taitung.

We arrived early and made our way, with time to spare, to the underground platform. In this part of the world, train stations are hushed places. The rules are followed and conversations discouraged.

Our ticket read 12:33, and at exactly 12:33 the 426 arrived. Two minutes later, we were on our way. Silent though it was - no clatter of wheels on the rails below - it was everything we'd hoped for. The Pacific lay to our left; mountains and fields stretched to our right. Occasionally, a town or cluster of homes broke the view. But mostly, it was just us and the 426, moving south, gazing out to sea.

The Tiin Tiin Inn

April 19

It's early, barely a soul on Xinsheng Road, and no one's at the front desk. I returned to our room after a walk to the 7-Eleven and a milk tea in hand. At the top of the stairs, a painting of a rabbit caught my eye. I liked it - the rabbit has a pack on its back, a fellow traveler. On the door to our room, a small wooden box. At 9:30 each morning, a local farmer drops off a warm bottle of goat milk, courtesy of the Inn.

Mickey, who works the front desk, gave us a walking map to aid in our exploration.

The Tiin Tiin Inn sits in the heart of Taitung, a city people come to for its slower pace. It has that feel. Kind of like Des Moines in the '60s, though Des Moines never had this many street vendors or scooters.

Travels with Pa

"If you can, stop by the Blue Dragonfly," Mickey told us.

"You won't regret it."

It sounded a bit racy, but we promised we'd try.

You never tire of the streets in Asia, the markets, the specialty shops, the wafting scents of something sizzling just out of sight. By mid-morning, we stopped at a place called Princeken and treated ourselves to a Firenze Daxi Matcha Green Tea (翡冷翠大溪抹茶綠茶) and a German Pudding Tart (德國布丁努). Back on the street, we wandered without direction, letting the hours lead the way, until noon arrived, and with it, the Blue Dragonfly.

Turns out it's not racy at all. In fact, it's legendary. Pa reminded me again of what Anthony Bourdain once said:

"Try everything once."

So we ordered the house special. Words don't do it justice.

After lunch, we took advantage of the rooftop laundry at the Inn, free to wash, just a dollar to dry, then stepped back out for a matinee. French, with Chinese subtitles. It didn't matter. Within twenty minutes, we both agreed: terrible. We left without regret.

It was a good day. Dinner was pork noodle soup and a cucumber salad. The streets had cooled, our spirits were full, and we slept well.

Tomorrow, we'll bike Taitung, bikes included, courtesy of the establishment.

Bashō

April 20

At ninety degrees, the streets of Taitung were too hot to explore, even by bike. So we headed out of town to ride the Forest Park Trail. For a while it skirted the sea, the breeze barely holding the heat at bay. Then we crossed a bridge and entered something new. Ocean gave way to lake, then marsh. Bike path became pathway. The landscape unfamiliar, not quite jungle, but exotic, nevertheless.

The last thing I packed before leaving home was a slim volume of Bashō's poetry. Bashō, the genius of brevity. I'd meant to save it for Japan, but couldn't wait. I've been savoring bits of the master's haiku these last few days.

Ebb tide –

willows

dip to mud.

Bashō had many disciples, but Dojo was among his favored. Of Bashō, Dojo once wrote:

"The master said, learn about a pine tree from a pine tree, and about a bamboo stalk from a bamboo stalk."

What would life look like, to be a Bashō? To take the time, and give attention, to the little things, the commonplace, that aren't so common after all.

On the ride back, the sea whispered its secrets.

Waves scaling

Sado Island –

heaven's stream.

Mazu – Goddess of the Sea

April 21

Lao-tzu, the "Old Master," probably wasn't the first Taoist. Like Homer, it's likely he never existed at all. But the earliest Taoist thoughts to survive are set down in the *Tao Te Ching* - The Book of the Way - and attributed to him:

The tao that can be told is not the eternal Tao.

The name that can be named is not the eternal Name …

Lao-tzu, like others before him, didn't require a god to start things off:

The Tao is like a well: used but never used up.

It is like the eternal void: filled with infinite possibilities.

It is hidden but always present.

I don't know who gave birth to it.

It is older than God.

And yet, humans have always struggled to live without gods. So in all cultures, everywhere, they arose from the depths, the heavens, and the stories we tell. Taoism now has many deities. But in Taiwan, especially for those who live by the sea, Mazu is the most revered.

Said to have been born human, Mazu demonstrated supernatural gifts from an early age and was later deified as the protector of seafarers, fishermen, and sailors.

Pa and I were fortunate to meet her at her temple in Taitung, the most prominent in the city, with the help of a personal guide. River, an expert in permaculture, was attending a nearby workshop in an indigenous community. She grew up Buddhist and Taoist. While she doesn't take all of her childhood teachings literally, she holds a deep respect for their underlying spiritual and psychological truths.

At the temple's entrance, we were each handed seven long incense sticks. We lit them, and one by one placed them at different altars throughout the temple. At each stop, a prayer was offered, or a request made. Pa, unfamiliar with incense from his own upbringing, said the ritual reminded him of the Stations of the Cross.

Mazu stood at the front and center, deservedly so, given her stature. But along the sides were other deities as well. Pa especially liked the old man, whose name I can't recall. Couples soon to marry come to him for guidance. If all goes well, they return with photos and notes of gratitude.

I once read a book by a scholar from Notre Dame who argued that the great value in studying the religious traditions of other cultures is that we return with insights for our own. All traditions offer a glimpse of ultimate reality.

But as the Buddha taught, or so I've been told:

Never mistake the finger for the moon.

In the Moment

April 22

We've stopped in Tainan. No particular reason, just that it's Taiwan's oldest city and happened to be on the way to Yingge.

Tainan began as a Dutch outpost, until a Chinese general, Koxinga, defeated the colonists in 1661. Pa thinks it's ridiculous that the Dutch strayed so far from home. After Koxinga's death, the Qing Dynasty took over, and then, in 1895, Japan gained control following the Sino-Japanese War. Turnabout being fair play, Tainan returned to Chinese governance after Japan's defeat in 1945.

And yet, for all that history, little of it remains visible, except for the abundance of Chinese and Japanese restaurants and the many Buddhist and Taoist temples.

After a breakfast of milk tea and Chinese pancakes, Pa and I went for a walk. We weren't looking for anything in particular, but you know how it goes. Something catches your eye, and you cross the street.

There was an alley, at the end of which a small building. But that wasn't it. Nearby, an intriguing structure, but that wasn't it either. I happened to glance back and saw a modest temple tucked out of sight. The attendant seemed to be having an easy day. Not wanting to disturb, we entered from the side, paid the fee, and stepped in.

With no one around, we took our time. Pa lingered near the front. I moved slowly between the figures. The bearded fellow on the right seemed to speak. A bit startled, I moved on, looking with normal eyes, as is customary.

But it happened again, and I lingered.

Then the realization - these aren't mere objects. I was reminded of *A Night at the Museum*. No matter where I turned, they were looking at me.

My mind turned to the Greeks and their Pantheon. The Taoists have their Pantheon as well, as do the Christians. Jung came to mind, and his collective unconscious. In the moment, I knew that they reside within each of us.

Pa Opens Up

April 23

We arrived in Yingge five hours and twenty minutes after departing Tainan. Unbeknownst to us, the young man who helped us at the 7-11 had booked us on a "local" - twenty-four stops between points A and B. It wasn't whisper quiet, but it was comfortable enough. More like an old Amtrak than a Bullet Train.

The car rocked back and forth, making its way through cities

Travels with Pa

and towns, past temples, green fields, and farmhouses. Unlike the coastal journey from Taipei to Taitung, there were no mountain vistas or ocean views to steal our attention. So Pa and I had time to talk.

I assumed we'd catch up, or maybe plan a little, with six weeks in Japan ahead. But Pa had something else in mind. He wanted to talk about his world, as he calls it.

"I apologize, Fred, for not telling you much," he began. "What I've shared about family and baseball is infinitesimal to all that's there."

I'd had questions, but hesitated to intrude. Pa's a private man.

"You see, we have a code. Not a rule, exactly, but an understanding. If we ever get the chance to visit our old home, this home, we're not to share too much. One of those rift-in-the-universe kind of things. Tell too much, and things on the other side might shift dramatically."

I could imagine. Though we're told truth can't hurt, maybe that's just a local belief.

"But all this talk about gods and goddesses, deities and saints - it's made me want to set the record straight, at least with you."

I was glad for it. I've had my doubts, and it meant something that he was willing to pull back the curtain.

"It's pretty simple, Fred. There's just before and after. No birth, no death. Just transition. Of course there are regions. Most who've left Earth stay with their own kind. There are exceptions, of course, but that's for another time."

Travels with Pa

I'd wondered about that too. Someday I'd like to meet an extra-terrestrial.

"And those revered ones, those in whose names so many have died, they're just like the rest of us."

I told Pa I hoped, when the time comes, to meet some of them

"You certainly will, though they're still as popular as they were on Earth. But we have events. We call them Holy Fairs, sort of like Woodstock, I've been told. By the way, I would've liked to go, but I was 93 at the time and couldn't make the trip."

I smiled and told him I would've liked to go too, but my senior year of high school was about to start.

"Anyway, people come from far and wide to the Holy Fairs. They're great. All the big ones are there, and a few you've never heard of, but who've got something interesting to say."

We were one stop from Yingge and had to gather our things.

"One last thing, Fred, everybody gets along there. Even the Big Names. Funny guys, some of them. A while back I overheard two of the biggest - hilarious."

Just after we stepped off the train, Pa added:

"Remind me to tell you about John Lennon. Nice fellow. Showed up not long after I did. The young man had it right:

Imagine there's no Heaven

It's easy if you try

No Hell below us

Above us only sky

Imagine all the people livin' for today…

Imagine there's no countries

It isn't hard to do

Nothin' to kill or die for

And no religion, too

Imagine all the people livin' life in peace…

except the Heaven part."

Most of the Time…

April 24

People come to Yingge for the pottery and ceramics. Known throughout Taiwan and beyond, kilns have been fired there for more than a century. Most visitors head to Old Street, where it's on full display.

Sometimes Pa and I go where the people are, to see what catches their eye, what feels good in their hands, and what they might take home.

But most of the time, we prefer the out-of-the-way shops and the Thin Places. We prefer to get a haircut and meet someone new.

We prefer to dine where the locals do, to stand in line and see what they're having, and order the same.

We prefer those who tidy up and put things in order, who pack up for the day and prepare for the next.

We prefer friends, fathers and sons, and families.

We prefer those who chill out, even when they ignore us.

And come evening, we prefer to chill out ourselves, on the rooftop garden of the Fish Hostel.

Heroes

April 25

We're back in Taipei, long enough to visit the National Palace Museum. Before moving on, Pa and I want to see its vast collection of ancient Chinese art and artifacts. We've splurged this time, staying at the Yusense Hotel, just a ten-minute walk down the road. We enjoyed our four days at Fish Hostel and Jerry's Maze, but life has its pleasures, and an undisturbed sleep is one of them.

It's early. Pa is still sleeping, and I've been thinking about heroes. Not the ancient ones. Not the super ones. Not even guys like Shrek (though I like him a lot), or young women like Moana, who's a fine role model for my granddaughters.

No, I'm thinking about the ordinary ones, extraordinary in their own way. Pa and I have met several since leaving home.

Travels with Pa

Like the retired woman from Singapore traveling with her husband. Not so quietly, she confided:

"Next time I'm leaving him behind. There's no adventure in him."

Or the retired woman from Manchester who sold everything to live on the road for a year.

Years ago, I read Joseph Campbell, the American comparative mythologist. His first book, *The Hero With a Thousand Faces*, remains a classic, inspiring many, including George Lucas who credited Campbell for planting the Star Wars seed.

Campbell wrote:

You must give up the life you planned in order to have the life that is waiting for you.

So Marco, the young man we met in Nepal, gave up a successful job in Germany to trek the Himalayas. He's staying on to work with and learn from an indigenous community near Bandipur.

Luisa quit a good job too. She's not sure what comes next, but after Nepal, she's thinking about moving to Bulgaria to practice as a naturopath.

There's Raghav, who took a chance, pursuing his dream at Green Chwadi rather than practicing law or taking a safe job with the government or an NGO.

And Lama Sir, who works for little so the students at Treveni School can pursue their dreams.

And Sugat, Deepak, and Ujjwal - each with families, each following their own path rather than society's.

Travels with Pa

Campbell taught that there are stages in the Hero's Journey, each with its challenges.

Like the 40-year-old from Chicago we met in Pokhara. He turned his back on his father's lucrative business, not knowing what lies ahead.

"But whatever it is," he told us, "it will be mine."

Or the 20-year-old from Atlanta who dropped out of pre-med to learn sustainable farming in the foothills of the Annapurna. He chose not to follow in his physician father's footsteps.

We spoke with a young woman from Croatia who didn't leave home until a few years ago. She had the opportunity to study in China, but the prospect seemed daunting. It wasn't until she asked herself:

"If not now, then when?"

that she was able to cross the threshold.

And yesterday, before leaving Fish Hostel, we listened to a young man from Taichung. He'd been staying in Yingge nearly two months.

"I'm trying to redefine myself."

When I asked what that meant, he said:

"I love my parents. They've given me much. But I don't want to be a teacher like my father. When I talk with him, he seems to listen, but then he says it's our duty in life to be responsible."

He spoke of the pressure to not let his father down, even if it means not living his own life.

Travels with Pa

It's so difficult, but I want a life too.

Just before leaving, I shared with the young man the lyrics to Cat Stevens' Father and Son:

Father:

It's not time to make a change,

Just relax, take it easy

You're still young, that's your fault,

There's so much you have to know

Find a girl, settle down,

If you want you can marry

Look at me, I am old, but I'm happy

I was once like you are now, and I know it's not easy,

To be calm when you've found something going on

But take your time, think a lot,

Why, think of everything you've got

For you will still be here tomorrow, but your dreams may not.

Son:

How can I try to explain, when I do he turns away again

Travels with Pa

It's always been the same, same old story

From the moment I could talk I was ordered to listen

Now there's a way and I know that I have to go away

I know I have to go

All the times that I cried, keeping all the things I knew inside,

It's hard, but it's harder to ignore it

If they were right, I'd agree, but it's them they know not me

Now there's a way and I know that I have to go away

I know I have to go.

As Pa and I rode the local back to Taipei, we thought of the young man at Fish Hostel, and hoped he would heed the call.

Addendum

We have not even to risk the adventure alone,

for the heroes of all time have gone before us.

The labyrinth is thoroughly known …

we have only to follow the thread of the hero path.

And where we had thought to find an abomination

we shall find a God.

And where we had thought to slay another

we shall slay ourselves.

Where we had thought to travel outward

we shall come to the center of our own existence.

And where we had thought to be alone

we shall be with all the world.

    -Joseph Campbell

A Brief History Lesson, And a Little Art

April 26

It's an interesting story, often bloody, as to how China's greatest art treasures ended up in Taipei.

The first chapter is simple enough. For centuries, China was a land of dynasties. The last of these was the Great Qing, who ruled from 1636 to 1912. Politics aside, the Qing were known to be greedy folk, hoarding the art of the people, some of it dating back to 6,000 B.C.E.

In 1894, the Qing got into it with Japan and lost, ceding Taiwan as part of the peace agreement.

Then, in 1899, a secret society known as the "Harmonious Fist", better known as the "Boxers", began slaughtering foreigners. The Boxers had the support of Empress Cixi, which didn't end well. Eight European countries sent troops to put down what became known as the Boxer Rebellion. The Empress ended up on the losing side, and the harsh sanctions that followed permanently weakened the Qing.

In 1911, Dr. Sun Yat-sen, a Western-educated reformer, led what would become known as the Wuchang Uprising. Within months, fifteen provinces declared independence from the Qing. A year later, Dr. Sun took power, and the "Republic of China" was born. But the story wasn't over.

In 1921, the "Communist Party of China" was founded, largely in response to dissatisfaction with the government's failure to stand up for Chinese interests in the Treaty of Versailles.

By 1927, Chiang Kai-shek, leader of the Nationalist Party, had taken charge. He ordered a brutal purge of Communists, leading to the deaths of millions. Out of the chaos, the opposing "Red Army" was born.

In 1928, Chiang officially took over for Dr. Sun and set out to unify China, seizing territory from warlords and consolidating power.

Then came 1931, and the Chinese Civil War. While the Nationalists and Communists fought for control, Japan saw its opening, invading Manchuria and later capturing Shanghai and Nanjing in 1937.

For the next eight years, China and Japan remained locked in a brutal stalemate, until Japan's defeat in World War II. As part of the postwar settlement, Taiwan was returned to China (remember, it had been handed over to Japan back in 1894).

But peace didn't last. Chinese soldiers clashed with Taiwanese

Travels with Pa

citizens, sparking violence, and Chiang sent in more troops. Meanwhile, the Communists gained ground on the mainland.

In 1949, the Communist Party declared victory, establishing the "People's Republic of China." Two months later, Chiang Kai-shek fled to Taiwan with two million soldiers, set up a provisional government, and claimed to be the only legitimate ruler of all China.

And what of all the art that Dr. Sun had recovered from the Qing in 1912? Chiang took it with him to Taiwan. That's how it ended up in Taipei, at the National Palace Museum. And yesterday, Pa and I got a glimpse.

It's overwhelming. Millennia of beauty and craftsmanship gathered under one roof.

As usual, our tastes differed. I was drawn to the paintings and scrolls. Pa preferred the older pieces, the ones he could touch and hold, had they but let him.

CHAPTER ELEVEN
Japan

A Little Different

April 27

Stepping off the plane at Fukuoka International, it felt different. Pa noticed too. Quieter for sure. There was no pushing or cutting in line, and passing through immigration was effortless, though I did leave my cap on the counter. Five minutes later, a young woman caught up with us and returned it.

As good as the 7-Elevens are throughout Asia, Japan is said to have the best, and their egg salad sandwiches, the best in the world. There wasn't food service on Air Taiwan, so we stopped at the first 7-Eleven we could find. It was adjacent to an ATM and well-stocked, with an entire shelf devoted to egg salad. We exited with a sandwich and a green tea, paid for with yen.

Taking a nearby seat, we met a young man from the Netherlands, halfway through his egg salad.

"Best there is," he said with a smile. "I eat them slowly. Savor them. They go down like ice cream."

He was right. We went back in for a second.

Check-in at Hostel TOKI was 4:00 p.m., so we opted for the hour-long walk rather than take a bus.

Word is that Fukuoka is laid back. Pa and I felt it immediately. Tree-lined streets. People and pigeons picnicking side by side. Pickup soccer, pitching practice, socializing, sunbathing, and napping after lunch. Crossing the street, no one goes until everyone goes. Though we weren't hungry, we stopped for a salad, different from the house salad back home. The house music played Brahms, then Stan Getz on sax.

And the bicycles. Everywhere. With right of way over all other manner of conveyance. It's quite different from Bangkok, Hong Kong, and Taipei, where motorcycles and scooters rule the road.

After checking in at Hostel TOKI, we walked the streets again, unlike any we'd walked elsewhere.

A Walking Meditation

April 28

Pa was always a walker. Nearly every morning he'd walk from the big house on Penn Avenue to his office on the west side of the river. He hasn't complained once about any walk we've taken. So over coffee, I suggested we walk the four miles to Ōhori-kōen Garden. It's on the north side of the city and was designed using landscape techniques from the Middle Ages. Knowing Pa tends to be more medieval than modern, I figured he'd be up for it.

"When do we start?" he said.

By 10:00, we were walking at a brisk pace.

Each walk is different. You never know who might show up. This morning, it was Thich Nhat Hanh:

Walking meditation is a practice to bring body and mind together. When we walk in a mindful way, we bring our body and our mind back together. Wherever we walk, whether it's on the street or at the market, we are walking on the earth and so we are in a holy sanctuary.

Thay's calming words slowed us down. Fruits and vegetables looked fresher. Parks and power lines each provided pleasure. Structures and streams complemented one another, suggesting that beauty is what brings inner peace.

Thay spoke again:

When we walk reverently, we generate the energies of mindfulness and of peace.

Stopping at the entrance to an elementary school, we were greeted by the statue of a young boy. Pa wondered aloud when a young mind should be introduced to beauty, and to meditation. We agreed it should begin in childhood.

He posed a second question:

Should the aesthetic experience inform meditation, or should meditation direct the aesthetic experience?

A bit of a silly question, I thought, but Pa was in a philosophical mood.

"I'm going with meditation," I said. "It provides the necessary foundation."

He was ready to argue, but before he could, we arrived at Ōhorikōen Garden, and the question was answered.

The *Garden*, after all, came before all else. Nature's innocence. Its intelligence. Before lights were needed to show the way, before bridges were built to get us from here to there. Long before there was a path - or a way - that might define us.

Pausing to listen to the fall of water, we felt something settle inside. But near the exit, Pa expressed a quiet regret:

I'm sorry that, later in life when I had the opportunity, I didn't live a simpler one, closer to nature.

On the walk back, we drifted into our own thoughts, caught up in our individual needs and desires.

Hita

April 29

We're on the afternoon bus to Hita, a city of 65,000, about 72 kilometers southeast of Fukuoka. Locals call it "the Kyoto of Kyushu" - a smaller version of Japan's ancient capital., and Kyushu, the third largest of Japan's five main islands.

Having recently watched the Netflix series *Age of the Samurai*, Pa and I know a little about Hita's history.

The warlord Toyotomi Hideyoshi captured Hita in 1593, fortified it, and made it his base for conquering all of Kyushu, a key step toward unifying Japan after a century of civil war. A decade later, in 1603, Hideyoshi passed control to Tokugawa Ieyasu, who became the first shogun of the Edo Period.

Two years after taking power, Tokugawa "resigned" in favor of his son Hidetada. But like many a shogun before and after, he continued to rule from the shadows.

For the next 260 years, the Tokugawa clan held sway over Japan, closing it off from most of the outside world. The lone exception was Dejima, an artificial island in Nagasaki harbor.

Dutch traders were permitted to live on Dejima under strict oversight. The Tokugawa saw them as more interested in commerce than in conversion or conquest, a sentiment Pa agreed with wholeheartedly.

Other than that, we don't know much else about Hita. But we've read that its clean mountain water contributes to some of Japan's finest beer. We'll find out.

Reminders

May 1

It's Golden Week in Japan, four national holidays packed into seven days. It began Saturday with the birthday of the late Emperor Shōwa, Hirohito. Wednesday is Constitution Day (*Kenpō Kinenbi*), marking the 1947 ratification of the post-war constitution. Thursday brings Greenery Day (*Midori no Hi*), honoring nature. And Friday is Children's Day (*Kodomo no Hi*), a celebration of childhood.

We first heard about Golden Week a few days ago, along with its implications. Many businesses close, banks included. Travel surges. Trains, buses, rental cars - everything books quickly. Hotels, homestays, even hostels become scarce.

We had planned to visit Nagasaki this week, and reserved a room for five nights. But we couldn't get there. We looked into Beppu, just two hours from Hita, but couldn't find a place for last night. Thankfully, the kind folks at Hotel Caffel Hina offered us an extra night.

"It's all good," as they say.

The delay gave us a beautiful sunny day to explore. So after breakfast, an hour in the public bath, and a massage, Pa and I set out with a map in hand.

Hita sits off the beaten path. Even during Golden Week, its streets are quiet. The Old Town road stretches just two blocks. Beyond it, a canal. We followed it until we reached a bridge. And you know how it goes, sometimes when you cross a bridge, the world feels different. Black and white, and shades of gray, can offer a clarity that colors sometimes don't.

Eventually we came upon a park. It reminded me of the grandkids, and the many hours spent in parks back home. A small stone statue looked just like Freddie in his bib. An altar nearby held figurines Nora, Lorelei, and Grace would love.

Down the road was a school, and a ballgame underway. Liam has a tournament this weekend. He's quite good. Past the school, another park, this one with a big black train engine on display. I took a photo and sent it to Oliver. He loves trains.

A few blocks later, we saw children at play. In that moment, I saw them all: Nora, Lorelei, Oliver, Grace, Freddie, Charlotte –

as if the streets of Hita were welcoming them too.

We stopped by the station to buy tickets to Beppu. Out front stood a statue of Eren Yeager, the hero of *Attack on Titan*. He reminded me of Liam, whose birthday is today. I'm sorry I won't be with him, but grateful for FaceTime so I can still join the party.

Pilgrimage

May 2

Leaving the familiar, you take a left, then a right, because that's where the river is, and the bridge, with its threshold to a different life, and an island you must go to, and a climb that's required, and from where you'd come from, you barely see it, but there's a path, with signposts at times, but often not, and strange things in the woods -landmarks and walkways to entries where permission is granted, and you marvel at shapes, forms, structures, and the culture from which they arose.

There's an enclosure - you approach, and inside the reminders of a different land, with a different wisdom, and a different people, whose faith is different, and can't be yours.

You want to stay but bid goodbye, descending as you must, taking the same path, though different, onto the same bridge, and the well-marked way, arriving at the station just in time to cross the threshold for another journey, to a different land where, at the end, you realize that life is but a pilgrimage.

Travels with Pa

Pilgrim

I bow to the lark, and its tiny, lifted silhouette, fluttering before infinity.

I promise myself to the mountain, and to the foundation from which my future comes.

I make my vow to the stream flowing beneath, and to the water falling toward all thirst,

and I pledge myself to the sea to which it goes, and to the mercy of my disappearance,

and though I may be left alone, or abandoned by the unyielding present,

or orphaned in some far unspoken place,

I will speak with a voice of loyalty and faith to the far shore, where everything

turns to arrival, if only in the sound of falling waves, and I will listen

with sincere and attentive eyes and ears for a final invitation, so that I can

be that note half-heard in the flying lark song, or that tint on a far mountain,

brushed with the subtle grey of dawn, even a river gone by still *looking, as if it hasn't,*

or an ocean heard only as the sound of waves falling and falling, and falling,,

my eyes closing with them into some undeserved nothing,

even as they give up their strength on the sand.

    -David Whyte

Above It All

May 3

We're staying at Guest House Rojiura. Nothing special, but it's clean, the shower's hot, and the price is right. It's tucked back on a quiet street, a little house next door, a rabbit around the corner, and a phone booth in case I lose my charger, or something worse.

There's a young woman at Rojiura. She asked about our plans for the day, to which we replied we had none. A resident of Osaka, she visits Beppu every year and knows a thing or two.

"You must visit Mt. Tsurumi," she said. "I go every time. Take the No. 1 bus to the base. Then ride the cable car to the top. When you arrive," she added with a smile, "you will be above it all."

We walked the sunny way to the station. At Pa's suggestion, Freddie joined us, he is our namesake, after all.

Travels with Pa

"And besides," said Pa, "you're never too young to go on an adventure."

Though it's a long way up, Freddie enjoyed every minute of the ride. And as we slowed to dock, he announced, rather emphatically:

"Again!!!"

The young woman was right. From the top, it seemed we could see forever. We took our time looking around, but Freddie eventually grew restless. Pa suggested a hike. Of the two possible trails, we weren't sure which to choose. But Freddie knew and we followed his lead.

Not long after, a second decision was needed.

"Fred and Freddie," Pa said, "there are times when it's good to test oneself. This is one of them."

The vote was unanimous. We pressed on - into the woods, then above them, and into them again. There we came upon a path, which led to a pillar, beyond which stood a sentry, and a strange land.

I was hesitant to proceed, but Pa was firm. "We've come this far."

So we moved forward, into a sacred place of tiny statues. Stern in some respects, but friendly in others, Freddie took to them right away.

After a time, we came to a marker with a message we couldn't decipher. Yet somehow, Pa knew its meaning and quoted Joseph Campbell:

Travels with Pa

We have not even to risk the adventure alone,

for the heroes of all time have gone before us.

The labyrinth is thoroughly known,

we have only to follow the thread of the hero path.

And where we had thought to be alone,

we shall be with all the world ...

Beyond the marker was a precipice - the air rarefied. The sky luminous. The walk down was easy. And soon, a signpost and a path returned us to our world. Back on firm ground, Pa looked up, then pointed toward the summit.

"It's good, at times," he said, "to visit the high places. To get above it all."

2 Hours And A Bike

May 4

Phil sent me a photo, which I like for the colors, and that I'm in the land of the Rising Sun. But mostly I like it because Phil sent it. He frequently does. Sometimes they're of his bicycle, or of him and Grace, or Julia and Grace. Whatever photos he sends, they're always thoughtful and lift my spirits.

Phil's the biker in the family. No one else comes close. It was in 2021 that he rode 20,000 miles plus, almost all of them on his trusted one-speed. Five years ago today he was in the second week of his TransAmerica Ride - Yorktown, VA to San Francis-

Travels with Pa

co. With Julia's blessing, and his boss's consent, he'd taken two months off to fulfill a dream. You're never too old to go on an adventure, you know. On that day, Phil was biking in Kentucky from Hazard to McKee. Having outrun a dog or two, he met a kindly officer, and they became best of friends. I like it that Phil enjoys a chance encounter and a memorable conversation.

I used to be a biker, not like Phil mind you, but I put some miles down. Phil's photos got me in the mood, so I rented a bike, a one-speed with a battery for assistance. I say "I" rented a bike because Pa declined to accompany me, preferring to keep his feet on the ground. And there wasn't a bike with a seat for Freddie.

Beppu sits at the tip of Kyushu Island, and on the sea. More specifically, it's on the south shore of Beppu Bay which separates Beppu from Yawatahma and Shikoku Island. Being on the Bay, I looked for a bike path and easily found one. In the habit of stopping along the way with Pa, there was much to see - art in the park, markers of memory and reverence, people enjoying the day, alone or with friends. Boats too, and walkways to them. Thresholds for some I imagine, going on a long voyage. After a time, the trail ran out, but there were back streets, with delights worthy of pause, reminders of beauty's passing, and of life's brevity.

On the ride back, Mt. Tsurumi loomed in the distance, and an old Peter Mayer song came to mind:

Suddenly I saw life from the brink,

I watched an age pass me by in a wink,

For just one heartbeat,

Travels with Pa

I believed I could think,

Like a mountain.

Mountain, we measure our lives

By tens and twenty years only,

Teach us the ways of a million-year mind,

What a million-year heart

Could be hoping.

And oh if I'm wise,

I will strive and I'll pray,

To turn a tick in time into a day,

And lead this poor

Picture-flash life in that way,

Like a mountain.

Heavy stuff. It's interesting how a single image can change your mood. But then a photo from Phil arrived, and a reminder that life is in the moment.

Little Things

May 5

It's our tenth day, and still much to see. But impressions have been made.

Japan, like the rest of the world has been overrun by modernity. Some of it good. Fast trains. Efficient cars. The modern conveniences of kitchen and bath. But even a foreigner can experience nostalgia for what's no longer. Take the art of years ago, when there was no clutter or bravado.

I was reading about Haiku, and came across a passage from D.T. Suzuki, the late Zen monk and scholar:

When a feeling reaches its highest pitch, we remain silent, even 17 syllables may be too many. Japanese artists, influenced by the way of Zen, tend to use the fewest words or strokes of brush to express their feelings. When they are too fully expressed no room for suggestion is possible, and suggestibility is the secret of the Japanese arts.

It appears that's been lost … but cultural remnants do remain.

The little shrines, with their details and strange delights overhead. The temples, open to everyone, and ever reverent. Public hand basins and quiet parks manifest a lingering civility, while love of tidiness, gardens, and flowers express a subtle sensitivity. Candy is still found in tiny shops, and prayerful people walk the streets. Even car and home are minimal and complementary.

And here in Beppu, at our Airbnb, efficiency and simplicity are bedfellows.

Travels with Pa

There was a child went forth ...

May 6

Today is *Kodomo* - Children's Day - the last of Golden Week's four holidays. I'm thinking of my children and my grandchildren, as Pa is of his. But being in Beppu, we're thinking of those close at hand as well.

The best friends, the kids on bikes, the brother and sisters, soccer players, baseball players, and those just learning to play.

Walt Whitman never had a child or children, at least none that ever stepped forth, but having been one, he knew something of them:

There was a child went forth every day,

and the first object he looked upon

and received with wonder

or pity or love or dread,

that object he became,

and that object became part of him

for the day or a certain part of the day,

or for many years

or stretching cycles of years ...

I don't know if philosopher Arthur Schopenhauer ever had children, but he knew something of the importance of parenting,

Travels with Pa

having been parented himself

The experiences and illuminations of childhood and early youth become in later life the types, standards and patterns of all subsequent knowledge and experience - the categories according to which all later things are classified - though not always consciously. And so in our childhood years the foundation is laid of our later view of the world. There, with its superficiality or depth, it will unfold and be fulfilled, though not essentially changed.

Whitman had a difficult father. Though he wrote little of his father, on occasion he alluded to him:

The strata of colored clouds,

the horizon's edge,

the flying seacrow,

the fragrance of salt marsh and shore mud;

These became part of that child who went forth every day,

and who now goes and will always go forth every day.

And these become of him or her

that peruses them now.

And so they're celebrating Children's Day here in Beppu, and throughout Japan. This Day, it seems, should be the equal of Earth Day, and celebrated Everywhere.

Travels with Pa

On The Road To Mt Aso

May 7

Pa and I enjoyed our stay in Beppu. How could we not. The mountains, the sea, the good food and friendly people, the leisurely walks. It's likely we'll return for a day or two, having yet to experience even one of the city's many onsens. But we were itching to get on the road and explore Kyushu Island to the south. The valleys and mountains, Mt Aso in particular.

There's a tension that exists when one travels - between getting to know a place and discovering the new on the road. It's akin to what we all experience at different times and in different ways. The need for both autonomy and family; solitude and fellowship. If we have the good fortunate to have some equal measure of both, we must consider ourselves blessed.

Anyway, we rented a car for ten days, as the hidden places on the Island are difficult to get to otherwise. With Golden Week hovering over everything, there were no cars available in Beppu. But Avis in nearby Oita had what we needed. So we hopped on a local and enjoyed the twenty minute ride.

A young woman at Avis patiently educated us, and by noon we were on the road - the left side of the road - with the first of many mountains straight ahead and Mt Aso two hours beyond. What happens though, whether walking or driving, is that places along the way have their own agenda and need for attention.

The little towns tucked in the foothills, the tiny shrines that accompany them, and the bridges needed to get to them. Coming upon another bridge, we deviated from our intended route, and explored on foot the little world beyond. But with Mt Aso our goal, we couldn't linger.

Pa, ever observant, spoke a short time later and said it was again time to pull over and onto a small lane that had appeared.

It was worth a stop - rice fields and ponds, stunning even under cloudy skies. Of course we had to move on, as time was slipping away, but mid-way back to the lane's beginning, there was a small shrine hidden in the greenery, marking the way to a path, leading to its own little world of farmland and green fields, creatures great and small.

Our day might have been complete, yet still, there was light enough for Mt Aso. So back to the car we went, but rooftops called for attention. Near enough to cause little delay, we walked in their direction, but on the right was a whisper, a gate to be more precise. And knowing, we bowed to pass under pausing at the poetry etched in stone, before making the ascent, believing the climb would do us good.

At the top, however, was a marker, pointing to a semblance of a path, which led to another ascent, where we paused before bowing and crossing the threshold.

There was a stone sentry, of course, as there should be at the entrance to such places, and we offered our due respect before proceeding.

Soon enough however, we were halted, recognizing in the moment that before us was hallowed ground. If you've ever been to such a place, you know there's a feeling that arises, difficult to express absent poetry or song. So we bowed our heads in silence. But faintly, as if carried by the breeze, lyrics by Peter Mayer arrived:

When I was a boy each week

We would go to church

And pay attention to the priest

He would read the holy word

And consecrate the holy bread

And everyone would kneel and bow

Today the only difference is

Everything is holy now …

And Pa and I acknowledged the truth of it, and proceeded slowly, moving, so as to no longer disturb. We walked to the other side, its own country in this little world we'd stumbled upon, where ancestors offer wisdom to all who all would listen.

Believing we'd been sufficiently prepared, we approached the shrine, tiptoeing gently until the final steps, where we found them to be much too narrow for our Western feet. There was no hurry. Mt Aso could wait for another day. But rain began to fall, so we retreated, looking back a last time at the great beings providing shade and protection over it all.

Just before crossing, we dipped our fingers in the shallow well, Peter Mayer at our side:

Travels with Pa

When holy water was rare at best

It barely wet my fingertips

But now I have to hold my breath

Like I'm swimming in a sea of it

It used to be a world half there

Heaven's second rate hand-me-down

But I walk it with a reverent air

Cause everything is holy now ...

Descending, we bowed again, then Pa, Peter and I walked back to the car.

This morning outside I stood

And saw a red-winged bird

Shining like a burning bush

Singing like a scripture verse

It made me want to bow my head

I remember when church let out

How things have changed since then

Everything is holy now

It used to be a world half-there

Heaven's second rate hand-me-down

But I walk it with a reverent air

Cause everything is holy now.

Onsen Day

May 8

The rain that began as we descended from the Shrine followed us all the way to Kurokawa and the Hostel Aso Base. Through the night it continued, a downpour at times, pausing at others, providing hope for a cloudless sky in the morning. But it wasn't to be.

Pa, ever practical, suggested we get to know our new way station and perhaps visit an onsen. I've come to appreciate Pa's outlook. Though highs and lows don't exist within his emotional range, his refined Stoicism makes him well suited as a traveling companion.

The Aso Base is welcoming, Japanese in its taste and simplicity. There's no food on site, but tea and coffee can be had any time of day or night. Pa and I both agree that the bed is as comfortable as any we've slept on. There's a quiet gentleman at the front desk, about forty, efficient in his tasks. I've approached him a few times and come to like him. He's an old soul. Pa and I believe that a deep Shinto lineage resides within him.

At about noon, the rain had become mist so we inquired if there might be an onsen nearby. For the uninitiated, an onsen is a natural hot spring bath. Heated by underground volcanic activity, they're found all over Japan. Beppu's many onsens are heated by eight separate hot springs. Kurokawa has just one spring, but it serves a handful of onsens. The man at the desk told us the best happens to be the closest, just a short distance from Aso Base.

"The Aso Bachu Onsen is family owned and generally only visited by locals. It's only 400 yen but you must take your own towel. Take a right out of the parking lot. Walk five minutes, no more. You will see the statue of Usopp, a popular manga character with a long nose and slingshot. It can't be missed. Take a left at the station, a right onto the lane, then the first left, and you're there."

We followed his directions to the letter and were greeted by two women with slippers who assisted us with the machine that dispenses entry tickets. They were sweet women, grandmotherly. Once my belongings were stored in our locker, the women escorted us to an inner entrance, beyond which only men are allowed. We didn't take photos thereafter as there were at least six patrons present at all times we were there.

Had I to do it over again, I'd own an onsen rather than be a lawyer. Pa and I are convinced that onsens contribute to a stable society far better than our judicial system. You can see it in the men as they prepare, still tense from the outside world. But then they shower, sit on tiny stools and pour warm buckets of water over head and body. Most proceed to the sauna and sit in silence with their brethren, far longer than Pa and I could tolerate. Next is the large hot bath, where they either sit on the side, or step in and recline, just their heads above water. Nearly all stop for a dip in the cold pool before showering a second time and dressing. We followed the routine as best we could.

Once back in the changing room, we observed the demeanor of those who came after. It was a "communal re-birth."

Japan isn't cursed with alcoholism and addiction to the extent most western countries are. I have to wonder if an onsen in every American neighborhood might go a long way toward solving our problems.

Mt Aso

May 9

What we knew of Mt Aso was sketchy at best, but there was sufficient sun when we left Kurokawa that we were confident we'd get to see it up close.

It was an easy climb in the rental car, the early going reminiscent of the Swiss Alps - grasslands, pastures, and all. The twists and turns were several but soon we were in high country where great trees called for our attention. Not wanting to ignore, we walked among them for a time, listening as they bowed to tell their stories. Resuming the climb, we wondered if Basho, pilgrim poet that he was, had visited these parts.

Clouds –

a chance to dodge

moon-viewing.

Travels with Pa

After a time, we came upon an entry but chose to drive past to avoid the traffic. We'd been told the mountain could be approached by walking a small valley to the west. Finding it, we did, and were rewarded with little things at our feet.

Come, see real

flowers

of this painful world.

Atop the mushroom –

who knows from where –

a leaf!

Clouds drifted in for a time,

Spring – through

morning mist,

what mountain's there?

 but fled shortly after, revealing a trail to our left.

Sudden sun upon

the mountain path,

plum scent.

Mid-way up, we got our first glimpse, and at the top, a second and better one. Descending on the far side, there was a lake and then a path that offered even better views. Reaching its end, we returned and visited a small museum devoted solely to Mt Aso. To our surprise, we learned that what we'd observed was not Mt

Travels with Pa

Aso but, instead, Mt Nakadake.

Seeking assistance, a friendly man at the information desk came to our aid, explaining as best he could that Mt Aso is one great mountain and within its perimeter is Mt Nakadake, the most active of five volcanos. He added that due to shifting winds, we could get no closer. Lingering for a time, we began the drive toward Minamiaso where we hoped to find lodging for the night.

Thanks to Booking.com we found a pleasant place on the outskirts of Minamiaso. Mr. Kawasaki, the proprietor and much like the gentleman in Kurokawa, took our information and showed us to our room. Later we asked if he had a dining recommendation. He did, and provided us a map.

It was a pleasant evening, with much to see, but distracted as we were, we lost our way until coming upon Township Bakery, which was all we could have asked for. Not knowing what to order, the owner was quite helpful and her recommendation delicious. Just as we finished, she brought us a surprise. Thoughtful as it was, to call it tasteless would be a compliment. After two bites, I quickly wrapped the remainder in a napkin and hid it in my coat pocket.

Of course I fibbed, and told her it was the best dessert I'd had in a very long time.

Travels with Pa

Three Pillars

May 10

It's said that the Three Pillars of Zen are Teaching, Practice, and Enlightenment. For Lao-tze, the Three Pillars - he called them the Great Treasures - are Simplicity, Patience and Compassion. I don't know that the Japanese have Three Pillars as such, but Pa and I are convinced that they must be Shinto, Fish and Rice.

As we were saying our good-byes to Mr. Kawasaki, he inquired of our plans. It's a question Pa and I have grown accustomed to. Sometimes we have a plan, but most often not. Having a plan can leave one feeling at the end of the day that something was missed or not accomplished. Aspirations, on the other hand, if not realized can be added to the list of "maybe or maybe nots".

So our response to Mr. Kawasaki was that we had a map and were considering a drive to the coast. Taking a look, he made a suggestion:

"You might stop at Kamishikimi Kumanoimasu Shrine. It's not out of your way, and would be worth your effort."

We thanked Mr. Kawasaki and told him we might do just that. And we did.

Shinto

I used to think of Shinto as a relic of the Japanese past, like Latin in the Catholic Church - ritualistic, preserved, but no longer lived. To our surprise, it's very alive. Those we've spoken to attest to its influence on their daily lives. And, according to one scholar:

While its origins date back 2500 years to the indigenous Yayoi, Shinto remains the consciousness underlying the Japanese mentality, the foundation for its culture and values.

Though just 20km from Mr. Kawasaki's, the drive to Kamishikimi Kumanoimasu Shrine was a slow one, the scenery making it difficult to pay attention to the road. But once there, our attention focused on the climb. Pa and I have come to realize that the Japanese find value in making it difficult to access their Sacred Places - the getting there as important as the destination. Once you've arrived, out of breath and yet relaxed, you're attentive to what's before you.

We stayed a while, observing those coming and going, some curious and some pilgrims. It seemed that even those with an itinerary were moved to a place of reverence.

Fish

Back on the road, we set our course for the coast. But a bridge we crossed caught our attention. We parked to take a photo then returned to find that two cyclists had arrived in our absence. Following them into *Umaya River Fish Dishes,* we placed our order, not quite sure of what. A few minutes later our server walked past with a net. Shortly after she returned with a sizable fish in hand. Over the next few minutes we observed the process, the result quite delicious.

Rice

Still intent on reaching the coast, we continued our drive, stopping once for fuel and an ice cream bar. Across the street, however, was a sign that caught our eye. So off we went in search of the *Sugayama Rice Terraces*. Along the way was evidence that we were in rice country and soon we were notified by Google Maps that we'd arrived. Unsure as to Google's accuracy, we approached a fellow with a large camera who assured us we were in the right place.

Taking a few photos ourselves, we followed him to a spot he said was even better. But his interest was a native weed which seemed to delight him. He encouraged us to observe it in the same manner. He then asked if he could take my picture. I agreed, provided I could take his.

Our friendly chat pleased him and he suggested that we accompany him further. Regrettably, we declined as we had a long drive ahead. Masking his disappointment as best he could, he wished us well.

We never made it to the coast, stopping for the night in Taketa. But it had been a good day - learning about Shinto, Fish and Rice - the Three Pillars of Japan.

The Potters' Village

May 11

Kyushu Island to the west, is a mountainous area ill-suited for

Travels with Pa

growing rice. So centuries ago, farmers became artisans after discovering that its forests, streams and clay were ideal for pottery. In planning our trip to Nagasaki, Pa and I learned that the village of Imari is particularly well known for its superb style.

While watching The Age of Samurai, we learned that the Japanese in the 1590s invaded Korea en route to China, hoping to conquer it. The Koreans resisted, and the invasion ultimately failed. What we didn't learn was that the invaders took many Korean potters hostage, returning to Japan with them as captives, intent on making ceramics a major industry. Sadly, the potters were never permitted to reunite with their families - suggesting a dark side of the Japanese character.

Imari has several nice shops, but we discovered that the real work is done in Okawachiyama, a village 6km up into the mountains. The "Potters' Village" it's called.

We arrived after most shops had closed, but finding a few open, we visited. There was a small matcha bowl I liked a lot, but $600 was beyond our budget. Exiting, we crossed a bridge that spans one of two streams, and came upon small workshops with kilns and the fuel required for firing.

Later we came to a second bridge, where a contraption had been constructed, powered by water that flowed into the spoons of great levers, resting until the water's weight was too great to bear - the purpose of which confounded both Pa and me.

Beyond that place was a cemetery and Tokomuen Grave, The Tomb of the Potters. The grave is built from the tombstones of 900 potters who spent their lives in the village - many born in Korea or descended from those first brought here as captives.

Travels with Pa

Piece of Cake

May 12

We've been staying at Mom's House, a little place down the beach from Shimonakano Fishing Port. There's not much at the port, which may be why Google had never heard of it. And that's what makes it so nice. There's just Ikitsuki Island and then South Korea, not more than a stone's throw to the west.

The couple running Mom's Place are nice too. Young and learning the business, they're very enthusiastic. It would be nice to visit them when I'm 80 - see how they're doing. When I told Jen I wanted to travel around the world after I turned 70, she responded that perhaps I could wait until I turned 80. I think I'll take that as a challenge. Pa won't be able to come along, having been granted his one furlough, but perhaps we can petition for an exception.

Having planned to leave at sunrise for Nagasaki, we found that the weather had changed dramatically over night. It seemed appropriate, as we'd be visiting the Atomic Bomb Museum and the site where the bomb exploded. It would be a somber day, a day without sunshine.

After leaving Mom's we drove to the port to see what was going on. The same boats were there, and the fisherman we'd seen the morning before. There was something timeless about the scene.

Yesterday we visited the Matsuura Historical Museum in Hirado. We'd heard there'd be a Tea Ceremony at 2:00. On arrival, we were told that it wouldn't take place. No explanation given. That was ok, it's their place. When we first arrived at the museum, the gentleman at the counter shot out of his chair, ran out the door of his small enclosure and around, showed me where to place my shoes, then handed me a pair of slippers. Tradition, custom, timelessness.

It was such a pleasant afternoon that we didn't feel like staying inside for another history lesson. The man behind the counter suggested we visit the Tea House. It wasn't open, but he said we could look around, at no charge. 125 years old, it had stood the test of time.

Back to this morning and our drive to the mainland. Crossing over the bridge, we stopped to look back at the Island. Two days can go by in the blink of an eye, or time can slow down to an easy stroll.

About an hour from Nagasaki, we stopped at a toll booth, and soon learned we'd mistakenly chosen the "ETC" line. We had cash but no way to pay. A Japanese fellow appeared on the remote screen but we weren't able to communicate. The line growing longer behind us, a young woman appeared, having surmised our predicament.

For a good five minutes she tried to talk some sense into the man on the screen, then suggested we pull ahead and park to the right. Directing us to stay put, she returned to the scene and continued negotiations on our behalf. Returning, she got in on the passenger side, took my iPhone with its Google Maps, and demonstrated where we could stop and pay in cash. Moved by her kindness, I took both of her hands and held back tears. With a most beautiful smile, she graciously accepted my thanks and replied simply,

"Piece of cake. Safe journey."

And went on her way.

Nagasaki

May 13

Nagasaki, surrounded on three sides by mountains and a colorful history of 374 years.

Nagasaki, where the curtain of history opened with the arrival of Portuguese ships in 1571.

Nagasaki, Japan's only open port from 1641 to 1859.

Nagasaki, 240,000 of its residents greeted the summer morning of August 9, 1945.

At 11:02am an atomic bomb exploded over the city, three days after the first atomic bomb exploded over Hiroshima. A clock was found in a house near Sanno Shinto Shrine, 800 meters from hypocenter. The flash of heat generated by the bomb caused fires that grew into a raging conflagration, centering in the Urakami district, then extending 3.5 kilometers south. It ultimately reduced one-third of the city to ashes. The bomb, the fires, and the lingering radiation killed 73,884 and injured 74,909 through the end of 1945. Others suffered and died for years after.

Travels with Pa

What has happened?

What has happened to the people?

Please do not forget.

Please tell others.

VOICES FROM NAGASAKI

Fuiio Tsuimoto, five years old at the time of the bombing:

I am now a 4th grade pupil at Yamazato Primary School. The school ground has been cleared. None of my friends know that so many children were cremated here. I sometimes recall that day. I squat down on the spot where my mother was cremated and touch the ground. And when I scratch it with a bamboo stick, chips of black charcoal appear. And I can see my mother's face floating faintly in the soil.

Michiko Ogino, ten years old at the time of the bombing:

My two-year old sister was crying hysterically, trapped under the fallen house. The beam was so heavy. The sailors tried to lift it but went away saying, "It's no use." Suddenly I saw someone running toward us. It was a woman. She was naked and her body was purple. "Mother!" Now we thought everything would be al-right. Our neighbor tried to lift the beam but it did not budge. "It's impossible," he said. "There's just no helping it." He bowed deeply in apology and went away. The fires were approaching quickly. Mother's face went pale. She looked down, and my sister peered up with fear-stricken eyes. Mother scanned the beam again, then slid her shoulder under it and heaved upward with all the strength in her body. The beam rose with a crack and my sister's legs came free. But mother sank exhausted to the ground. She had been out in the field picking eggplants for lunch when the bomb exploded. Her hair was red and frizzled. Her skin was burned and festering all over her body. The skin had ripped right off the shoulder she had applied to the beam. The muscle was visible and blood was streaming out. She soon began to writhe in agony, and she died that night.

Sachiko Yamaguchi, nine years old at the time of the bombing:

"What on earth has happened?" said my mother, holding her baby tightly in her arms. "Is it the end of the world?" We knelt in the air-raid shelter, praying to God with all our hearts. Injured people came into the shelter one after another muttering, "Urakami is a sea of fire." What was going to become of us? Since the shelter was bad for the baby, we departed for the house of an acquaintance in Mikumi-gochi. But when we arrived in Mikumi-gochi we found that the houses in the valley had also been destroyed. Where could we go to find a house in which my mother and her newborn baby could rest? Large groups of people were huddling together, trembling in the shade of the mountain and other places. Desperately thirsty, I went to draw water but found an oil-like substance floating all over it. People told me that the oil had rained down from the sky. But I wanted a drink so badly that I gulped the water down just as it was.

Travels with Pa

Sumako Fukuda:

I was to receive treatment as an "atomic bomb patient." I felt as though I had been branded with a fearful stigma, a stigma that would not come off no matter how hard I tried to remove it No basic method of treatment had been found for atomic bomb disease. The atomic bomb survivors were deeply and tragically convinced that no amount of treatment would ever provide a cure. Designation as a sufferer of atomic bomb disease brought that conviction to the surface as a burning stigma. As soon as the stigma was branded we began to live under a whole new set of values, abandoning ourselves to a life of hopeless solitude until death. This is a world that shuts out all the joy and hope of an ordinary human existence, a world of despair and isolation painted over in black.

Dr. Tatsuichiro Akizuki:

"Concentric circles of death Concentric circles of the devil." I found myself mumbling these words as I drew a mental map of the city of Nagasaki. Death seemed literally to be fanning out in concentric circles with each passing day. Today people living in houses up to that point died. Seeing this, I would be correct to assume that the people living another 100 meters up the hillside would die the following day. The ripples of death that expanded from the hypocenter soon began to consume people who had suffered only mild injuries or who seemed to have escaped unharmed. "There is still a long way before the circle of death reaches the hospital..." Living every day in trepidation about the expanding circle, I gathered people together and tugged at their hair. "Are you losing any hair?" I asked. The head nurse and all the nurses and patients shook their heads, showing an

expression that revealed neither anxiety nor freedom from anxiety. We were all suffering to some degree from a feeling of sickness. Our bodies were weakened by fatigue and diarrhea.

Man, 39 years old at the time of the bombing:

At the age of 40 I suddenly found myself without a family. That morning they saw me off with smiles when I left for work, but now I was alone in middle age. There are no words to describe this grief. Every day until the first anniversary of the bombing I sat in front of the pot containing the ashes of my eldest daughter (nine years old, grieving over the fact that I had survived. I could not even look at newspapers or magazines. Nor could I bear to go outside because it made me so sad to see children the same age as my own departed but unforgettable children. I lived day after day simply shedding tears and wondering when and how to commit suicide. The memories of that time are still etched clearly in my memory.

Nagasaki – 77 Years Later

May 14

Nagasaki is a small city, easy to walk. Not quite quaint, but with an old-town feel. Young families, kids walking home from school - none of them alive when the bomb exploded. And its harbor, with its modern skyline, still handles freight from around the world.

But the day of the blast, when so many were killed and just as many wounded, has not been forgotten. Visitors from all over come to pay their respects, to learn. Walk the area near the hypocenter, and you'll find reminders intended to last.

We attended the late Mass at Urakami Cathedral, standing on a small hill 500 meters northeast of the blast site. Begun in 1895 and completed in 1914, the cathedral was completely destroyed on that August morning in 1945 - all but a portion of the southern wall. It's since been rebuilt, but walking the grounds afterward, the reality presses in - nearly 9,000 Catholics perished in the bombing.

Pa and I talked about how hate and anger can pass from one generation to the next, sometimes for centuries. We wondered what it is about the people of Nagasaki that they have transformed their city of rubble into a city of peace.

The Dutch in Hirado

May 15

Pa is a funny guy. Not in the humorous sense exactly, though he does tell a good joke now and then, and he has a sharp eye for irony. By funny, I mean complex. A stoic by nature and temperament, he carries a sensitive soul, and his feelings can be hurt by the smallest unintended slight. Like the other day.

I don't think I've mentioned that when we were in Hirado, we visited the Dutch Trading Post. That was a big deal for Pa, and I told him I'd write about it. But then we moved on to Nagasaki, and the memories of Hirado began to fade. But not for Pa. He's immensely proud of his Dutch heritage and traces his roots back to Hendrik Van Leeuwen, born in Utrecht in 1630. When we visited the Trading Post and learned that the Dutch were present in Hirado during Hendrik's lifetime, Pa grew deeply sentimental. When I failed to tell that story, he felt forgotten.

So, though my memory is usually good for only a day, here's what I recall.

In 1600, the Dutch ship *De Liefde* landed in Bungo near Usuki, the first Dutch ship to reach Japan. Onboard were letters requesting that Dutch ships be allowed to establish a trading relationship. Things moved quickly. By 1609, two more Dutch ships had arrived in Hirado, entering through Usaka Bay.

On September 20 of that year, the Hirado Dutch Trading Post was formally established. It marked the beginning of Dutch Japanese trade relations that would last through the entire Edo period (1603–1868) and continue in some form to this day.

Trade between the two nations flourished, soon requiring larger storage facilities. Two warehouses were built, one in 1637, and another in 1639. The second, measuring 46 meters long and 13 meters wide, survived the centuries. Reconstructed, it now houses the museum we visited.

Flower Garden

May 16

Walking down the street, a woman, bent low, caught our eye.

Travels with Pa

She gestured, and without a word, pointed to a petal, then another, then motioned for me to touch one, as if to pass its energy on. I learned a lot in those brief moments.

As we walked on, Pa spoke of Bea and how much she loved flowers.

"Right now, her tulips would be coming up," he said. "All flowers were her friends, but tulips were her favorites."

Pa then confessed that it was only late in life that he grew fond of them. After he'd closed his practice and Bea became sick, he began to notice their beauty. And after her passing, he learned to care for them. Then he asked if we might visit a garden.

"I saw one on the map, at the base of Kuju Mountain. An easy drive from here."

He was right, and we arrived before noon.

Like Pa, I came to appreciate flowers late. For a long time, I told myself I'd spend the time when I was older.

It was quiet in the garden, spacious and seemingly ours alone. Little islands of delight gave way to trellises, which opened onto mountains of white, canopies of pink and green, and blankets of blue.

There was a bridge, and below it a stream. Along its edge, baskets of flowers lit the way.

I thought of the woman on the street, and her rose. And of Mary Oliver, a kindred spirit:

"When the roses speak, I pay attention...

Travels with Pa

"As long as we are able to be extravagant,

we will be hugely and damply extravagant.

Then we will drop foil by foil to the ground.

This is our unalterable task, and we do it joyfully.

And the roses went on,

Listen …

the heart-shackles are not, as you think,

death, illness, pain, unrequited hope,

not loneliness,

but lassitude, vainglory, fear, anxiety, and selfishness."

Their fragrance, all the while, rising from their blind bodies, made me spin with joy."

There is much to contemplate in a rose, whose true love is beauty - its momentary delicacy, its soft spiral meant to catch the eye, and its thorns meant to protect it from the hand that might pluck it.

Jigoku

May 17

We're back in Beppu, wanting to experience its hot springs - its *onsens*. Beppu, with more than 2,500, is Japan's hot spring capital. It was Golden Week when Pa and I were last here and the crowds kept us away. A normal year brings 60,000 during Japan's week of national holidays. It being the first since COVID, more than 100,000 came to town.

It's quieter now in this little city nestled on three sides by mountains of green, and stretching along the deep blue of Beppu Bay. There are onsens throughout Beppu and beyond, but most who come visit the Kannawa neighborhood where water gushes out at temperatures as high as 300 degrees.

Centuries ago when Beppu was a sleepy hamlet, the Kannawa area was described as "a cursed land of gas explosions, bubbling mud, and steaming waters." And the places where water exploded out of the ground were called "jigoku", the Japanese word for hell. Legend has it a Buddhist monk by the name of Ippen Shonin showed up and calmed the hells, allowing the people to enjoy the thermal waters.

Today, Kannawa is dotted with many hot springs and several Jigoku. Pa and I visited the one called Umi-Jigoku - Sea Hell. A hot spring 200 meters deep, its water is almost boiling. There's no getting in, but just to wander around is a delight. And at the end, there's a small pool, where the temperature is just right.

Pa wasn't satisfied, though, and asked if we could visit an onsen he'd heard of, 20 minutes into the mountains by bus.

It was a different place, off the beaten track. An older woman runs it, quite resourceful it appeared, as she's tapped into the thermal waters to generate electricity for distribution. Just beyond the mini power plant, is a trail that passes through a deep stand of elegant bamboo. And at the bottom of the steep hill, a little paradise where she's created a place of respite for those fortunate to find their way there.

Shrines

May 18

Beginning with Nepal, there have been shrines everywhere Pa and I have visited - Buddhist, Hindu, Taoist, and now Shinto. But there's something different about the shrines in Japan. They're more numerous, certainly. Their architecture, unique to the Shinto tradition. But it's more than that, though I couldn't put my finger on it at first.

What I've come to realize is that Shinto, and the shrines and temples that visibly express it, is woven into daily life in Japan. Despite modernization, Shinto lives in the blood. It's in the manner of eating and dress, in reverence for ancestor, elder, family, and stranger. And the shrines, they are not relics. They're where people still go - not just the older generation - to pray, to petition, to lay down burdens, to seek healing.

It's fascinating, and moving, to watch from a distance as a believer approaches a shrine. There's reverence and humility. And the intention to be transformed, if only for a moment.

There are shrines small enough to carry with you. Some that neighbors tend and honor. Shrines along the roadside that invite you in, ask you to pause, look around, get acquainted. Others, like the shrine to Dake, pull you into an aesthetic so Japanese, so

Shinto, that the world feels changed when you leave.

And then there are shrines of a different kind - primordial, you might say.

The path may look familiar at first, but as it narrows and the signs become unintelligible, you realize you've entered the realm of the impersonal. No gate or structure will greet you. You approach with reverence, look back - and a hand at the end of a branch, reaches out. You grasp it. And suddenly, you're in a shrine, a cathedral, only nature could construct.

And that's not all. For all things have a source.

You cross the stream again - for isn't it our task to seek that place of calm water, of myth and mystery? A place whose depths can't be plunged, but whose source we acknowledge but will never truly find.

But that's the journey.

Spring Fever

May 19

Pa has Spring Fever and has gone home. I knew it would happen - baseball, family reunions, and all.

"Not for long," he assured me.

His team has a tough stretch of games coming up, and they need his bat. More specifically, his hitting. Without him in the 4-spot, he says, it won't be easy for the hometown boys.

Travels with Pa

Quiet though he is, Pa doesn't lack self-confidence.

"And Stan Musial is going to coach us. He's a good friend, you know."

He then showed me a photo to prove it.

There's a big Van Liew reunion coming up as well. Pa says ancestors going all the way back to Utrecht will be there. There hasn't been a reunion of its kind in over a hundred years -long before Pa arrived.

"I can't miss it. I hope you understand, young man."

Of course I do, and told him so.

I like it when Pa calls me *young man* rather than *Fred*. It makes me feel younger than I am. Of course, age is irrelevant where he comes from.

Pa went on…

"I intend to be with you at the Finish Line. Besides, I promised Bea I'd return to our Iowa home one last time."

So Pa left in the night, leaving me to take the train to Kyoto. I've been looking forward to visiting the old capital, its shrines and temples, quiet neighbors, hidden nooks and crannies. But without Pa, it won't be the same. I can't say for sure, but I may not write much. Still, I'll take photos. I want to remember.

These days, more than ever, I take Paul and Art to heart:

And what a time it was

It was…

A time of innocence

A time of confidences...

Long ago, it must be...

I have a photograph

Preserve your memories

They're all that's left you.

Pilgrimage

May 20

It was odd at first, traveling without Pa, on the train to Kyoto without him to compare notes. But, and I don't want Pa to know this, in some ways it's liberating. So often we live with others in our head.

I got to thinking about the possible ways of being when abroad - tourist, traveler, pilgrim. It's easy to distinguish the latter two from the first. But traveler and pilgrim can appear to be the same.

Pa and I've been travelers, much as Whitman suggested:

Afoot and light-hearted I take to the open road,

Healthy, free, the world before me,

The long brown path before me leading wherever I choose.

Travels with Pa

But a pilgrim is one with a purpose, most likely a destination, like those who walk the Camino de Santiago.

I suggested to Pa, long before we arrived in Japan, that we walk a section of Shikoku's 88 Temple Pilgrimage. He wanted nothing of it. Far too much time on our feet and a different bed every night. So I put it to rest. While it's too late to walk the Temple route, I've been wondering if I might approach Kyoto as its own pilgrimage.

I've been carrying a slim guidebook - *Deep Kyoto Walks* - since leaving home. Opening it for the first time this morning, I read about the *Gojō-Zara area*, the first chapter.

When I say I read it, I mean I glided over it, having discovered that it's best not to spend much time with a guidebook. Not to read or research to the point where you're predisposed. Like I said, there are times when you don't want others in your head. A pilgrimage should be mine, not someone else's.

So I looked at the map, picked the Toyokuni Shrine as a destination, then put the map away. From there, I used Google Maps to get close, then turned it off. Keeping it on would shut the door on other possibilities.

You cross the Kamo River to get to the Gojō-Zara neighborhood. At first there's nothing special. A few restaurants, a park, pleasant homes. One time, I glanced to the left, and followed an alley to a little gem. Another time, I glanced to the right and followed, having learned that if I pass by, I might miss the path I was supposed to follow.

At the end, there was a left hand turn, and a woman appearing

Travels with Pa

from nowhere. I followed, believing she knew where she was going. Try as I might, I couldn't keep up. To my left was a welcoming shade tree, and a shrine beyond.

I entered into another world. To the left a bell, to the right the sound of voices. Straight ahead an open door. I thought I was alone, but yet sensed I was being watched. Her name is Akiko, wife of the Buddhist priest in whose Temple I stood. She greeted me warmly, explaining that a service was taking place. A member's mother had passed away 48 days ago.

Akiko invited me to look around, reminding me of the importance of remaining quiet. I whispered that I was sort of a Buddhist. While her English is limited, she seemed to understand and smiled. I told her my mother had wanted me to be a priest but that in my tradition priests aren't allowed to marry. She understood that as well. I didn't tell her that my mother, more than once, had told me that one day I'd be either the Pope or the President. Mothers are often delusional, particularly when it comes to sons.

At the end of our tour, she led me outside to the cemetery where we talked about ancestors and their importance to the Japanese. I told her about Pa. She understood.

The service ended and she had to go, inviting me to return later in the week to meet her husband.

On the walk back, I paused at the Toyokuni Shrine. Too many people. There were other impressive structures as well.

But there are times when only the back streets and alleys will satisfy.

Travels with Pa

Slow Travel

May 21

I started the day with a plan: Select a random chapter from *Deep Kyoto Walks*. Do a cursory read. Review the map in the Appendix. Identify one destination among several. Head out. *Across Purple Fields* sounded intriguing, with the Hanjō Shrine the first stop.

It's easy to linger at the Hibari Hostel, so I got a slow start, leaving shortly before noon. It wasn't long and a mild hunger set in. Nothing urgent, but it needed to be addressed on the way to the Shrine.

As fortune would have it, a little place appeared on the right, one that looked like where locals dine. At other times I might say that "I took a chance" but I've had nothing but delicious meals in Japan so I entered without hesitation. I didn't realize until I had a menu in hand that it was Chinese and almost everything offered was some variation of noodle soup. Having had it more than once, I ordered the large 大盛 for 950yen.

It wasn't a busy place, in fact "hurry" is most likely a foreign word. I liked that. It gave me the opportunity to observe the chef, who moved with an ease that belied his expertise. I admired him, though we never exchanged a word, or even a glance.

I have no idea how long I waited, as it wasn't a wait at all. But out of nowhere it seemed, the bowl appeared, and I soon found it to be the best soup of any I've had since leaving home. In fact to call it a soup does it an injustice. Had I been sick, it would have cured me.

And the little woman who did everything but cook, they don't make them like her anymore, at least back home. There was even something about the `way she handled my money and gave me change. She accepted it, as though I had made an offering

Back on the street, it was an easy afternoon, with no urgency. It carried over to the side streets, and the little houses, my gait slowing in sync with my surroundings. I observed a woman sweeping in front of a small shrine and left a small offering. Behind it was the Buddha, and to his right, a small cemetery where the ancestors reside.

On the street again, I took notice of the dwelling places, how they are shrines in their own right, constructed and landscaped in accordance with the Shinto aesthetic. By the time I emerged, I was no longer called to visit the Hanjō Shrine.

Turning the corner, I pulled out the map that Yusuke at the Hibari had given me. It had a list of nearby onsens. An hour in the waters of a hot spring seemed like the right thing.

Immersed in my map, a woman approached to see if I needed help. We talked for a while, during which I learned about the Japanese character system, how it's merged over the years with the Chinese, and how there are three related but distinct systems, all three of which she learned in school. After the instruction, she took hold of my map, selected an onsen she thought I'd like, gave me directions, and was on her way. Her name is Hide (He Day) and her directions right on. In ten minutes I was there and in ten minutes more had showered and was bathing.

On the way back, I was attracted to a little restaurant. Waiting for a table, I studied a painting on the wall. It seems that the Japanese have always traveled slowly.

On A Sunny Afternoon

May 22

I was thinking of Pa this morning - wondered how his team is doing and whether his eye is as good as ever. He says he hit over .400 last season, but there's no record of it. Still, he's not one to fib.

And I wondered what would interest him if he was here. I'm pretty sure he'd like Kyoto, its balance of progress and tradition. Having done some city planning in his younger days, he'd appreciate the public transportation system and the way the streets are laid out.

I got to looking at the subway map for places he'd want to visit. Near the end of the Green Line, and not far from the Shokubutsuen stop, is the Kyoto Botanical Garden. If Pa was here he'd choose to go there, though he'd probably get homesick thinking of Bea and spring flowers. As he's not, I could take a lot of pictures his return.

Pa has a nearly photographic memory, or so he says. As I can't recall him ever forgetting anything, I'll have to take it as fact. Anyway, I'd be sure to take enough so he could report back to Bea.

Travels with Pa

It being sunny, I walked the thirty minutes to Kyoto Station. On the Green Line by noon, I was off shortly after. A ten minute walk and 200 yen for entry and I was inside, greeted by a lovely lady.

It was quiet. There was a young bamboo grove, and an even younger stand. Some peonies, last of the season I imagined, and a pond with two young lovers.

I thought that was it until I emerged from a wooded area and came upon a different garden. It was quite something, a delight in fact. Endless flowers at the height of their glory.

Then I realized I wasn't alone. There was a photo bug, another, and another. An old painter, and a younger one. A young scholar, a young botanist, a couple of bird watchers, strollers, single and in tandem, more photo bugs, and a fellow - quite happy to just be alive. And there were a few at rest too, for what better place to be at rest. Pa would surely have joined them.

I left the people behind and entered a different garden - stepping back in time - a special place, one where spirits surely reside. On the far side, a woman in reverie.

Not wishing to disturb, I made my way back to where the people were.

I'm not an expert on gardens, but I do know what it is to be transported - and to have to return.

Travels with Pa

House Cleaning

May 23

Last evening, just before shutting things down for the night, Yusuke told me a priest was coming in the morning.

"He's going to exercise. You're welcome to join us."

I didn't think it odd. Hibari Hostel has a nice courtyard and the priest would likely lead willing guests in a Qigong session, or something similar.

I told Yusuke to count me in, then asked for specifics about the exercise.

"No, no. He's coming to do an exorcism."

"Oh my," I thought. Having been raised Catholic, I wondered who amongst us had evil spirits. And then wondered if there was any of us who didn't.

Yusuke explained further:

"Hibari shut down for COVID. The owner decided to retire and sold to a friend and his wife. They reopened in April and secured a priest to do a purification."

It all made sense, sort of. Anyway, I adjusted my itinerary, sketchy as it was, and arrived just as he started. For ten minutes he chanted, in ancient Japanese I assumed, then led us outside.

My room, "The Annex", was first. I wondered what the priest knew that I didn't. Next, we followed him upstairs, going room to room, all the while he shook his white paper *haraegushi*.

Travels with Pa

A brief note about the Shinto purification ritual (Harae - 祓). Like Catholics, Shinto priests exorcise to cast out unwanted spirits. Harae is a benevolent act, a blessing for people, places, and objects. I was told that in Japan it's a big deal when a new car is purchased. Anyway, with all the rooms purified, we returned downstairs for a brief ceremony, each of us handed a branch with green leaves and notes on white paper attached.

One by one, we approached the altar, bowed twice, clapped twice, bowed to the altar again, and then to the priest. I was last, the assumption being, I suppose, that if I first watched the others I might get it right when my turn came. Turns out the young priest is with the Matsuo-taisha Shrine. The same Shrine where the couple was married twenty years earlier.

After everyone was gone, I revisited my itinerary, foregoing the Saihjo-ji Temple, replacing it with the Matsuo-taisha Shrine. It took a while to get to there - the combination of bus, subway and train made it that.

Being late in the afternoon when I arrived, most of the day's visitors had left. I stopped at the ticket booth but the elderly gentleman wouldn't accept my yen.

"Too late. You visit for free."

I asked if should go to the right.

"Sorry. No can go. Off limits." And he pointed to the left.

Not knowing what I was missing, I was impressed with what I was allowed to see - the care, the craftsmanship, the reverence. It's said that the Westerner can never fathom the Eastern mind. I'm becoming convinced of that.

Travels with Pa

Too soon, a gong sounded, announcing it was time to leave. Returning to the entrance, and the old man, I asked if I might take a quick photo of what was to the right, offering my assurance that I wouldn't enter. He asked that I wait, left his assigned station, then gestured that I follow. We entered and he took me to a place where I might have a moment of peace.

Trusting me it seemed, he left me to enjoy without disturbing. Not wanting to delay the kind man, or anyone else, I kept my visit brief.

On the way out, I crossed over a bridge, pausing to enjoy the spring flowers. Everything is numinous in its own way, even the traffic.

Postscript

The point is not how unusual it all is.

The question is: how many times do we have to be touched before we're changed?

Toji

May 24

Kyoto Station, traffic central for Kyoto and the surrounding area, is a 30 minute walk from Hibari Hostel by the most direct route. 30 minutes is just right for beginning the day. This morning, however, I decided on a different route, not for the sake of exercise, but for a change of scenery.

Travels with Pa

Halfway along the Google path, I took a right and walked north until intersecting with the main line east out of the Station. With school kids just ahead, I followed, assuming they were on a field trip and the Station was also their destination. But to my dismay, they were going shopping. Not in the mood, I continued on, certain the Station wasn't far off, and it wasn't.

My plan, upon leaving the Hibari, was to choose one of the half dozen train lines and see where it might take me. It appeared the *Kintetsu* had chosen me, so I let it take the lead until a woman with the Railway approached and wondered if I needed help.

"Where do you want to go?" she asked.

I told her I wanted to ride the train and wondered if she had a suggestion.

"Have you been to Toji?"

I apologized and told her I knew nothing of it.

"Toji Temple is very famous, and not far down the line. You must visit it."

Not wanting to offend, I accepted her suggestion, after which she retrieved a paper map, circled the station, and led me to the platform gate, all for 270 yen. Safely on board, I and the others waited for the engineer to show up.

A minute later we were on our way. Disembarking two stops later, Toji was in sight, or so I thought.

The five story pagoda in front of me was just that, part of a much larger complex dating back 1400 years. I approached the main entrance where schoolgirls had gathered for a photo. I took one as well, and was called out. They were kind enough to oblige me a second photo, then insisted that a male friend include me in another. I have no idea why the interest.

Once inside, I realized that Toji is an extensive complex, and Kondo Hall, built in the 8th century and rebuilt in 1603, one of several impressive structures. And like the Matsumoto-taisha shrine, there were smaller, but no less impressive, gems scattered throughout. I stopped to photograph one of them, when a woman approached, politely took my camera, and told me where to stand. Before I could protest, or offer reciprocity, she was on her way.

After a time, I noticed that there wasn't a scrap of litter to be seen, and what had been in plain sight drew my attention - five or so volunteers grooming a rock enclosure - cleanliness being central to the Japanese character. Overseeing it all, the Buddha and one of his followers.

Rain was on its way, so I made my way back on the Kintetsu Line, then followed the path through Umekoji Park where I paused for three young men on their violins playing "Amazing Grace", and giving it their all.

Deer Park

May 25

Nara lies an hour south of Kyoto Station on the Kintetsu Line. Small in comparison to Japan's major cities, people flock there. I visited Nara several years ago. While the specifics had all but

Travels with Pa

disappeared, I never lost the feeling of the place.

Most visitors, if they only have a day, spend it at Nara Park, more commonly called "Deer Park". I was reminded that it gets its name from a legend.

In the 8th century, there was a Nara clan - the *Fujiwaras* - that invited a god from the *Kashmir* Shrine to visit. The god showed up riding on a white deer and ever since, locals have protected deer as divine messengers.

So the first thing you notice when you arrive are the deer, they're everywhere. They're not troublemakers, though when I was in line for an ice cream cone, one deftly lifted my park map from my back pocket. Certain he knew his way around better than I did, I grabbed it back.

There are other sights, including the Kohfukuji Temple and another Five Story Pagoda, both of which are favored by aspiring artists. As much as I enjoyed observing the deer, and the artists, I moved on in search of something quieter.

Taking a side path, I happened upon some locals content to be by themselves, and nearby Ara-ike Pond where solitude is welcomed, even honored. For a while I observed a fellow quite interested in something. Summoning the courage to approach, he looked up and explained, with gestures, that he's a bug collector. I would like to have learned from him, knowing little about bugs myself, but I bid farewell and climbed the hill in search of the Kasuga Trisha Shrine, a monument I recalled from my earlier visit.

Along the way, I observed a young boy treating a young lady to a horseback ride and some buddies passing the time with a soccer ball. But I was intent on my destination and finally arrived at the Shrine, like Matsuo-taisha and Toji, a complex of delights worthy of pause.

But longing for something quieter, I left the crowd behind and took to a path, centuries old for sure, designed to take the seeker away from the traffic, and into Thin Places.

What is necessary, after all, is only this: solitude, vast inner solitude. To walk inside yourself and meet no one for hours – that is what you must be able to attain. To be solitary as you were when you were a child, when the grownups walked around involved with matters that seemed large and important because they looked so busy and because you didn't understand a thing about what they were doing.

    - Rilke

Get Thee To An Onsen

May 26

Having set it aside for a couple of days, I decided to revisit *Deep Kyoto Walks*. Rather than consult the Table of Contents, I went straight to the Appendix, and the Maps. Each has its merits but No. 8 - Nishikikōji Market, seemed the most straightforward, and doable.

If I walked it start to finish, I think Pa would be proud of me, having followed through on an itinerary. Besides, by the time I got to the beginning, it would be lunch hour and it's the author's claim that " … the Eitarō has an excellent yuzu ramen."

The route was easy, too far to walk but not too far by bus.

Just a note, should you ever become addicted to Google Maps. Coupled with a good data plan, it's indispensable for walking a city, or anywhere for that matter. But what I've discovered in Kyoto is that it also provides everything needed for public transportation, including the walking route to get to where you hop on. There's another function I've come to love - the real time Blue Arrow. It points you in the right direction and keeps you there.

When I turned the corner, I knew I was close, but not how close. The Blue Arrow got me to the exact spot I needed to be, *just below the Irish Pub* as the author promised.

The Eitarō, being a favorite of the locals, is a busy place, requiring that I wait just inside the front door. The wait turned out to be fortuitous as there was a gentleman at the table next to me who had just finished his soup. As he approached the cashier, I asked what he thought of it.

"It's the best on the menu," he assured me. "You won't do any better."

So I ordered it, and he was right.

Leaving the Eitarō, I consulted the map, and called upon the Blue Arrow for stop 2. It was close by and I needed only to make my way to the entrance of the Nishikikōji Market. Once inside, the Daiyasu was immediately to my right. And, as the author predicted, the old man for whom the fish shop is named was hard at work. It was fascinating to observe him, but to linger at

Travels with Pa

the Nishikikōji Market means to risk being trampled.

It wasn't long and I spotted Nishiki Daimaru, known for its donuts, though on this day I was enticed by the matcha soft serve with chocolate sauce drizzled over it. Enjoying the treat immensely, I was optimistic, and assumed I would next be directed to exit the Market and make my way through a neighborhood of Shrines and Temples. But I was mistaken.

Consulting the map, and Google, I discovered that each of the remaining stops, except the last, were all within the Market. I was trapped. I didn't want to disappoint Pa, but I wanted to make it out alive. And there were 13 stops to go. My breathing accelerated and my chest began to seize. But I gritted my teeth, clenched my fists, and moved on.

As fortune would have it, the Inoue Tsukudani-te was permanently closed. And while the Uchida Tsukemono Nishi-ten did have some delicious looking fare, and Notoya was interesting enough. Google couldn't find Kanemats, Miki Keiran, and Shimamoto Nori Kanbutsu. Under other circumstances, I would have asked for directions. But I kept coaching myself: "Don't ask anyone, anything. Your life depends on it."

Now I understood Thoreau when he wrote:

"Most men lead lives of quiet desperation."

He was talking, I believe, about men "enlisted" to accompany a partner shopping.

But there was light, and a shrine in the distance. And as I neared it, a *Wendy's*. I thought I was going to vomit. But I held on and made it out, though from the looks of things, I was certain they'd be selling Chicken McNuggets.

The urge again, but then the voice, the one that never fails:

Get thee to an Onsen.

And I did.

And it was good.

The Japanese Soul

May 27

I spent the morning at Hōnen-in, a small Temple, a short way up the mountain slope on the eastern edge of Kyoto. A friend told me it's worth the effort getting there, and there would be few visitors. She was right on both counts.

A young man descended the steps shortly after I did, and we compared notes. 6'4" and angular, I was certain he was Dutch. Had been Pa been there, I would have been corrected before suggesting it. Introducing himself as *Louie,* the young man was quick to put me at ease, volunteering that there's Dutch on his mother's side, and that both sides of the family have always gotten along.

I sensed Louie to be a sensitive soul, my assumption confirmed as he described his walk through the Temple grounds. We agreed that there are temples and there is Hōnen.

Louie, by the way, is a graduate student from Paris, nearing the end of six months at a Tokyo university. He's been researching the sociological and psychological impact of the 2011 Fukushima nuclear disaster. It was fascinating to listen to him recount conversations he's had with survivors, particularly the elderly. Sadly, Louie has learned that the Japanese have little tolerance for those who've suffered psychological trauma. We wondered at the paradox between that insensitivity and the Japanese soul that for centuries has produced art and architecture as sensitive as any created throughout human history.

Named after Hōnen (1133-1212) the founder of the Jōdō-shū school of Buddhism, the Temple was established to honor him and his efforts to make Buddhism more accessible to the common people.

After Louie left, I retraced my steps to experience a second time Hōnen's sublime simplicity. Upon leaving, I paid a brief visit to the adjacent cemetery, to the ancestors, and the overseers.

On the return to Hibari Hostel, I wondered at this complex people, and what will become of its collective soul.

Kyoto Vignettes

May 28

It rained all day, a good "stay at home day" as Liam says. A day to sort through photos and put them in albums. There are several I didn't have a place for, but then it occurred to me to categorize them in a fashion that might make sense to those following along.

Travels with Pa

The Masters - Artist and architect Tadao Ando had a brilliant idea to reproduce eight masterpieces and display them in an outdoor garden. It's a wonderful experience to walk amongst them. Most of them I know. I'll do some research and identify the few I don't.

The Abbott - Just down the road from Hōnen-in Temple is a small Buddhist Temple, the Anraku-ji. It's a lovely place. The Abbott gives a talk every Sunday afternoon, after which milk tea and custard are served at a nominal price.

The Philosopher - There's a pleasant walk locals like to take known as the "Philosopher's Path". There's nothing spectacular along the way, which makes it special in some respects. It runs along a canal where the fish that got away make their home. If you're fortunate, you might see a young couple hoping to get away from it all, and a few steps behind, a mother. On the afternoon I walked the Path, there was a young philosopher immersed in Basho's *The Narrow Road To The Deep North*.

The Blacksmith - Makato Kawakami toils away in his village studio an hour to the east of Kyoto. But once a month he comes to town to display his art. After the crowd thinned, he was kind enough to give me a tour, finishing with his favorite piece.

The Map Makers - A bus, a subway, and another bus from Hibari is the Kyoto Library Archives. There's an exhibit of two to three hundred year old maps of Kyoto. And across the street, a quiet restaurant with a delicious Udon Noodle soup.

The Chef - Not to be outdone, is a little place a block from Hibari. The Chef serves up a wonderful fried chicken thigh lunch known throughout the neighborhood.

Uji

May 29

It's the start of the rainy season. And whatever is left of Typhoon Mawar when it reaches the mainland will likely mean wet weather until Pa and I fly home. But you count your blessings, and today being partly sunny is one of them.

I'd been wanting to visit Uji, a town mid-way between Kyoto and Nara, known for its matcha. I'm a believer in the green stuff, its flavor when prepared right, and its medicinal benefits no matter the naysayers. I wanted to visit Uji to taste the local matcha and perhaps participate in a tea ceremony. The pleasant day made it possible.

But before the matcha, it's important to know that Uji is also famous for its part in *The Tale of Genji*. The 1,200-year-old romance is considered a classic of Japanese literature, and walking about town is a reminder of that. There's a museum dedicated solely to the *Tale*, small but poignant in the ways it tells the story.

So there's the matcha and the *Tale*, but people visit Uji for other reasons as well, like to marvel at Byodo-in Temple. I've visited a few temples now. But Byodo, with its architectural design and stunning setting, captures the best of those I've seen. No matter the angle, it's the best angle possible. Even on a day when it seems half the students of Kyoto are visiting, it's still stunning.

But back to matcha. It is the primary tourist attraction, and it's what it does to ice cream that seems to be the big draw. Though

Travels with Pa

I would have liked to indulge, I really did want to taste authentic matcha in a setting designed just for it.

So I went looking and happened upon the Taiho-An ceremonial tea house, arriving at a time when there weren't other visitors. It made no difference to Fukiyo, my teacher, retired after years of instructing high schoolers on the basics of English grammar and composition. I wasn't allowed to photograph once Fukiyo's colleague had completed the preparation, but it's the feeling I'll hold onto, and the taste of the *wagashi* sweet, chewed slowly before the first sip.

Song of Tea

Lo Tung (790–835)

The first sip moistens my lips and throat

The second sip breaks my loneliness

The third sip revives my heavy mind, sparking some five thousand tomes inside

The fourth sip makes me slightly perspire, flushing through the pores every bit of worry

The fifth sip purifies my flesh and bones

The sixth sends me to the sages immortal

The seventh sip could not be drunk, only the cool wind rises in my sleeves

Travels with Pa

The Railway Man

May 30

My father was a railroad man. In his day, those who chose to be railroaders treated the traveler with utmost care. Every summer until high school, he put me on the night train to Omaha to visit my grandmother. I can still feel the attention given by the conductor as we journeyed through the dark, the little Swedish woman waiting at the far end.

The other day, I was on the train to Matsuo-taisha Shrine. Failing to pay attention, I got off a stop too soon. Realizing my mistake, I consulted Google Maps, which directed me to walk two minutes. I exited the station, recognized my error, and returned. Inside, I caught the attention of the man behind the counter, showed him my phone, and did my best to explain the situation.

He told me I would need to swipe my card again and pass through the turnstile. An absurdity, I thought, but I didn't want to make an issue of it.

Once on the other side, he summoned me.

"I issue a credit," he said kindly, and then commenced:

Step one: Look up something in little black book.

Step two: Retrieve blank paper.

Step three: Make note.

Step four: Consult computer.

Step five: Fill out green credit form.

Travels with Pa

Step six: Affix official stamp.

The kind Railway Man then explained what I was to do with the green form, none of which I understood. He pointed me to Platform 2, the same one from which I had departed minutes earlier. Once there, I learned the train for Matsuo-taisha Shrine would arrive in five minutes.

With time to spare, I walked down the ramp to take a photo, so I might remember. Then, a tap on the shoulder. It was the Railway Man, concerned I was still confused. He walked me back up the ramp and placed me in the exact spot where I was to wait.

A minute later, the train arrived, at the exact moment promised.

Poet David Whyte wrote:

Traveler, of all shelter

you'll ever find on the road,

even with those you know,

the stranger's love is best of all.

I don't know if that's true of the Japanese, having heard more than once that you never really know what they're thinking. But I've come to understand this much: if you respect their culture, they will treat you with care and deference.

For the traveler, that is love enough.

Travels with Pa

Middle of Nowhere

May 31

Some days you just want to ride the train, rest your legs, and allow the mind to wander. No maps, no images. You don't want a bullet train on such days. You want the rocking to and fro, the lurching, the sounds that come when steel touches steel.

Just yesterday I learned of Umeroii Kyotonisi Station. Ten minutes from Hibari, it sits back from Shichihommatsu-dori Street in such a way that you wouldn't notice it unless you'd been there before. Having discovered it, I thought I'd visit rather than walk another twenty minutes to Kyoto Station and the Tower. You can catch the Sagano Line at Umeroii and ride it beyond the city, beyond the houses, businesses, and power lines.

Most people on the Sagano Line get off at Saga-Arashiyama and stroll through the Bamboo Grove. On another day, I might have done the same. But this morning, that wasn't far enough. So I stayed on. We traveled for quite a while, and what I'd hoped would disappear did, giving way to dense forests. Eventually we stopped, and I stepped off, assuming we were at a station.

Turns out we were on the Hozu Gawa River Bridge, one tunnel behind, one ahead, and the river running beneath.

It was, in fact, a designated stop - Hozukyō. While not a station in the usual sense, there was a small machine to swipe my railway card, which allowed me to exit. A narrow road lay ahead. I followed it and came upon another bridge, at the far end of which was a road that was closed. A second one, to the right,

Travels with Pa

continued. Ten minutes further and a decision had to be made. I chose to descend into the Mizuo Gawa narrows, where it was cool, welcome relief from the heat of Kyoto.

I could have walked for miles, or so I told myself. But the road ended at the confluence of rivers. Steps led down to the water's edge, where the Hozu Gawa flowed to the left and the Mizuo Gawa to the right. I considered crossing, but there was no easy route. So I found a rock and sat.

It's good to find such resting places - to stop and listen, and nothing more.

After a time, I returned to the narrow road and was soon atop the Hozu Gawa River Bridge again, looking down to where I'd been. The blow of a whistle broke my reverie as my ride home approached.

Today is Walt Whitman's birthday. He'd be 204 had he lived longer. As the engineer set the brake, I thought of Walt and how he would have invited others to stop with him this day, were he looking down from the Hozu Gawa River Bridge.

Stop this day and night with me,

and you shall possess the origin of all poems,

you shall possess

the good of the earth and sun,

there are millions of suns left,

you shall no longer take things

at second or third hand,

nor look through the eyes of the dead,

nor feed on the spectres in books,

you shall not look through my eyes either,

nor take things from me,

you shall listen to all sides

and filter them for yourself.

Lessons

June 1

It rained and rained, and rained some more. At least 6 inches they say. But Hibari held up, and the rest of Kyoto too, from what I know. Still, it wasn't a day for temples or shrines, or hiking in the woods.

I considered the Railway Museum, the best in Japan according to reviews. But then a German woman staying at the Hibari recommended a tea ceremony she participated in earlier in the week. So I went online, found an opening at 3:00, and within the hour I was on the 208.

The ceremony took place in a century-old house, actually two houses attached, the one on the left, a story and a half. The one on the right, two stories. We were told that in the day of the samurai, commoners weren't permitted to live in two-story homes. To do so would enable them to look down on samurai passing by.

The "tea school" is run by Michiyo, a retired elementary school teacher, now an understudy in *chanoyu* (tea ceremony) to a renowned Kyoto master. Michiyo took four of us under her tutelage, a young woman from Vancouver, a second from Munich and her partner, a young man from Zurich. Just the right number for a group experience.

She began by teaching us the Japanese expression *ichi go ichi e*. One chance, one opportunity, holding our attention by reminding us that,

This time we have together is a one-time opportunity, so let us make the best of it.

She then demonstrated *seiza*, the nearly impossible act of kneeling with one's buttocks resting on the heels, and introduced a few basic terms: *chawan* (tea bowl), *chashaku* (tea scoop), and *chasen* (tea whisk).

After walking us through the process - *chawan*, *chashaku*, matcha, water, and *chasen* in concert, we ate the obligatory *wagashi*, the sweet that balances the slight bitterness of matcha.

I've been doing a simplified *chanoyu* for about eight years as part of a morning practice to lower my blood pressure but realized I'm still a novice. But Michiyo praised us all, and at the end imparted a final lesson:

Travels with Pa

Wa Kei Sei Jaku

和 敬 清 寂

Wa – the importance of harmony in Tea

Kei – the importance of respect

Sei – the importance of purity

Jaku – the importance of selfless tranquility

In the evening, the rain having abated, I took a walk and discovered a little place near Hibari. It was open, and I was led to a table by one of two women, and handed a menu, in Japanese of course. I didn't feel like pulling out Google Translate so I went with what was at the top, figuring it must be a local favorite.

Seated near the action, I got a primer in another "process."

It started with a hot griddle, then a ladle of a thin batter, upon which was placed a mound of cabbage, a handful of grilled beef, a heap of udon noodles with a light sauce drizzled over it all, followed by the shaping it into a pancake, then a second sauce, sort of a BBQ.

The whole thing was placed on my tabletop griddle and seasoned. The two women, sisters I learned, didn't like how I was doing it, so they took over and cut it up, sort of like a pizza. It was quite incredible. I did my best to eat it all, but in the end took half of it home for a second meal.

As I was about to settle up, they asked where I was from and how old I was. To both questions I answered truthfully. They then asked that I guess their ages as well. My response giving rise to glee. Sensing that they wanted to take me home, I gave them a handsome tip and quickly made my way to the door, promising to return.

Take-no-Michi Trail

June 4

The rain ended, leaving in its wake flooding throughout Japan. Rail service was all but shut down. But in the morning on my walk to Kyoto Station, there were no signs of it, and business as usual as I approached. But upon entering, I was witness to hundreds of cancelled ticket holders lined up to rebook. It was fascinating to observe them, stoic as only the Japanese are. It could easily have been the British Museum or the Louvre where decorum is not imposed but welcomed.

It was my good fortune to have no destination other than the Take-no-Michi Trail on the far side of Kyoto. The city's subway system was unaffected by the washouts and I need only make my way through the crowd to the Tokaido-Sanyo Line, ride 3 stops to Katsuragawa Station, then walk 3km to the trailhead.

Exiting the Katsuragawa, I was soon in an area with little traffic. Not far beyond was groomed farmland watered by a canal system, through which traversed an elevated walkway. Being an Iowa boy, it was an interesting contrast.

It wasn't long, and I had passed through the long rows of cabbage, spinach, carrots, and onions and it into a quiet neighborhood of tiny homes with their tiny gardens. Passing through it, I began an ascent along a rock path through a thick forest, eventually arriving at the Take-no-Michi Bamboo Trail.

To walk through the tall, slender, elegant beings, is to be transported to a time when we had yet to desecrate our planet.

Sadly, the trail ended and a cemetery emerged, its stone markers reaching to the sky as though petitioning the gods for another chance.

Descending the opposite side of the mountain, I came upon a simple rock garden, no entrance permitted, and for good reason. Groomed in the way of the Zen masters, it invited contemplation and repose, just as the Take-no-Michi Trail had.

Hibari

June 5

I never intended to spend the last 6 weeks in Japan. After Thailand, my plan was to fly to Ho Chi Minh City, travel to the north and back, then continue on to Fukuoka mid-May. But as wonderful as Vietnam is said to be, a month of 95-100 degree days with humidity just as high, suggested a visit some other time.

The beauty of long-term travel is you need not be locked in. A suggestion from a fellow traveler, a change in the weather, can set you on a new and unanticipated course. So, just because I could, I substituted a few weeks in Vietnam with Hong Kong and Taiwan. That left 6 weeks in the Land of the Rising Sun, none of which I regret.

Travels with Pa

I'll write tomorrow or the next day on my overall impressions - before Pa returns on Thursday for the flight home. For now, I want to share something of my Kyoto neighborhood and of the Hibari Hostel, my home these past two weeks.

Why Hibari? It was cheap I guess, and simple, and not far from Kyoto Station. Other than that, I knew nothing else. When I arrived by train in Kyoto, I walked the thirty minutes, surprised that the final blocks were in the heart of a warehouse district. An odd location, I thought, for my days in the ancient Capital. Then I arrived at the Hibari, an island amid the commerce.

I fell in love with the place, consistent as it is with my simple needs and nature. And I found a friend in Yusuke, the manager, who every few days replaced the flowers on the wall of my tiny room. As the days passed, and I explored Kyoto's sights, I grew quite fond of my neighborhood, its oddities and treasures, not the least of which is the vending machine next door, with its chilled milk coffee, slightly sweetened.

I'll miss Kyoto, my neighborhood and most especially, the Hibari. I believe I'll return someday, good fortune permitting. But all things, the best included, come to an end.

Alice And The Rabbit

June 7

I often think of rabbits, projecting onto them an intelligence they probably don't possess. Nevertheless, I imagine that the cute, cuddly surface of rabbit belies a wisdom and cunning from

Travels with Pa

which we might learn. I suppose others have a different creature for which they are particularly fond, beyond the beloved cat or dog. But for me, it's the rabbit.

Then I arrived in Japan, and learned it's the Year of the Rabbit, and I see them everywhere. Of course, the sight of them leads me to Alice and her child's wisdom that has taught many.

A few years ago, I revisited Mr. Carroll's classic. I wonder now if that reacquaintance planted the seed for my dream to travel around the world. It was a silly dream some suggested. And from time to time in the months before leaving, I thought they might be right. It would certainly be easier to stay home rather than follow that rabbit down the hole.

When I get back, and have adjusted to Iowa time and home, I'll likely reflect on my time away and write something of it. But for now, as I look out my window on the 9th floor of the Tokyo Airport Hilton, I'm thinking of Alice and of her experiences.

Oh, how I wish I could shut up like a telescope! I think I could, if I only knew how to begin.

"For you see, so many out-of-the-way things had happened lately, that Alice had begun to think that very few things indeed were really impossible."

    -Lewis Carroll

I'm thinking of friends and acquaintances in their 60's and 70's who might follow their own rabbit down its own hole, if only they knew how to begin.

By the way, Pa has decided not to fly back with me. He says his one trip was enough.

"Baseball and the good company of family and friends are all I need. Besides, when the time is right, there will likely be other worlds I will want to visit."

- Fred T. Van Liew

AFTERWORD

I returned home on June 9 and over the weekend everyone stopped by at one time or another. It was wonderful and Jen made it special. In the days and weeks that followed I've reconnected with family, perhaps relating in a different way than before. I had missed them all, more than I realized in the moment. Being with them again, oftentimes just watching, reinforced their monumental importance to my life.

It's been a transition, though. Not painful but considerable. I'm still processing what happens to a mind when it's allowed to observe the world, and itself, outside the usual boxes of comfort, certainty and safety. To engage in conversation day in and day out with one's interior, that formless presence which sees and knows everything. Perhaps in another blog I'll explore the pros and cons of traveling solo versus with a partner or group - to move about without itinerary, agenda or deadline.

They say the brain is plastic and that we can nurture that plasticity well into our later years. "Before and after" brain MRIs might not reveal changes but it feels at times as if mine has been rewired. I don't know if that's a good thing, having to live in the world as it is. I'm fortunate, I suppose, to be at that age where less is expected and I become more invisible.

But the question for now, is how to balance the desire for community / family / intimacy with the need for autonomy. I wonder if most people, after the time of child rearing and work life, ask themselves the question.

I'm aware more than ever that stretches of solitude are necessary for my well-being, as is home life. Discerning the proper

Travels with Pa

measure of each is the challenge.

For the past several years I've done restorative justice work in Maine, initially with the Portland Center for Restorative Justice and now with the Cumberland County District Attorney. After being home four weeks, I headed east, making my way over three days rather than the customary two. I was surprised, though not entirely, that by slowing down I could revisit that quiet space I had known for many months.

It helped that I exited I-90 mid-way across the state of New York, took the back roads to the Hudson River, drove at a snail's pace across Vermont, and stopped for an afternoon to hike the Champney Falls trail in New Hampshire.

Having been in Maine for nine days now, I camped near South Freeport at a HipCamp site, down the road from Winslow Park where I shower for free and walk the beach trail. I've had lunch at the newly opened South Freeport Market, stayed at the Black Elephant Hostel on Hampshire Street in downtown Portland, and with friends who live near the shore of Portland's Back Cove with sweet Emma.

I've taken in the Hokusai exhibit, had Thai food with a good friend at the Green Elephant, and walked the Eastern Promenade on a sunny afternoon. Tomorrow I'll facilitate a restorative dialogue in a criminal case referred by the Maine Attorney General's office then meet with the Cumberland County District Attorney to chart a restorative justice course for the next twelve months.

Moving forward, striking the right balance will likely not require months away, though I'd do it all over again and every day would be a new one, just as before.

Travels with Pa

Yesterday morning after showering, I met a young man from Quebec City who had just arrived in his camper. We struck up a conversation, one thing leading to the next. I enjoyed it immensely, just as I had enjoyed chance conversations while away.

I learned a little of Serge's life or work, but what I've taken from our chance meeting is the story he shared about Boucar Diouf from Senegal, now a Canadian.

Boucar - scientist, teacher, writer, comedian, and storyteller - tells of a man who arrived at the entry gate of a remote village in the Ivory Coast. The man was met by an elder who inquired of his needs.

City Fellow: "I'm from the city where there's noise, chaos, and conflicts."

Wise Man: "You've come to the right place. Our village is just the same."

And so the City Fellow moved on, continuing his search.

Sometime later, another man arrived at the village and was greeted by the Wise Man.

Wise Man: "Tell me, what are your needs?"

Traveler: "I have no needs as I'm a mere traveler. All along the way I've been met by good people who've treated me with great kindness. I'm in search of more of the same."

Wise Man: "You've come to the right place. Please come in.

POSTSCRIPT

Travel Notes from the Steps of St. George

April 25, 2024

I was in Old Cairo, a year after Japan, about to climb the steps to the Church of St. George when a guide approached, a pleasant man in his thirties. He asked if I might like to join his group. He wasn't pushy, like some, or insistent in any way. I considered, though I'm not one to walk about with ten or twenty people, led by a man, or woman, stick held high in hand, pennant at the top.

As his group wasn't full, Yassar and I talked. Compared notes. I listened. He listened. In the end, I decided to go alone, at my own pace, seeing what I wanted to see. But my traveler's mind had been set in motion, offering up what I've learned through trial, and much error, and might be of value to others.

These are the thoughts that floated up as I ascended the steps leading to the Church of St. George:

- Decide before you leave, do you want to be a tourist or a traveler?

- Consider going alone. If that's not possible, at least go alone for an hour or two each day. When you're with another - spouse, partner, friend - it's more difficult to have "your experience".

- Rarely use a guide. You're not likely to remember what they tell you.

Travels with Pa

- Have a good smart phone, (I prefer Apple) with a good data plan, but turn off the cellular as much as possible.
- Carry a charger.
- Take photos, but not too many.
- Take notes.
- Become skilled with dictation.
- Keep a journal, paper or on your phone.
- Do research ahead of time. Do research after.
- Use Apps, and become familiar with them before you leave.
- Use Google maps when you're lost, knowing that getting lost can often be the best thing.
- Rome2Rio is nice for getting the big picture.
- Try not to book lodging before you leave, except the first night or two. You want to have an adventure, not be locked into an itinerary. Try to go for at least two weeks.
- Use an App like Omio for booking buses and trains city to city.
- Consider Uber rather than a taxi. There's no haggling. These days, Uber is much safer and you know ahead of time what you're going to pay.
- Use a good flight search engine. Skyscanner is my favorite.
- Google Translate is invaluable, as is Currency Pro for conversion.
- World Clock tells you at a glance what time it is at home, and elsewhere.

Travels with Pa

- Cross busy streets with a local, just a step behind.
- Take photos of signs. Learn from them. They often provide excellent information.
- When necessary, have a good driver. A good driver can tell you much on the way.
- Wear good sandals in a warm country, not running shoes
- Wear nondescript travel pants with lots of zippered pockets, not blue jeans.
- Always pack light.
- Always drink lots of water.
- Avoid the heat of the day if possible
- Don't take cruises, unless it's the boat ride you came for.
- Don't take tour buses with people like yourself. You can talk with Americans back home.
- Always take your time. It's about quality not quantity. Have two or three good experiences a day. Far better than checking off a list of 8 or 10.
- Be curious.
- Engage.
- Know that you know very little.
- Get off the beaten track.
- Seek out the quiet places.
- Trust your intuition.
- Trust humanity.

Travels with Pa

- And above all, never underestimate the quiet power of your presence:

Humanity is like an enormous spider web, so that if you touch it anywhere, you set the whole thing trembling. As you move around this world, and act with kindness, or with indifference, or with hostility, toward the people you meet, you too are setting the great spider web a-tremble. The life that you touch for good or ill will touch another life, and that in turn another, until who knows where the trembling stops or in what far place and time your touch will be felt. Our lives are linked together. No one is an island.

-Frederick Buechner

About the Authors

Fred Van Liew is a retired lawyer, restorative justice practitioner, and writer. He lives with his wife in Des Moines, Iowa, with his five children and eight grandchildren nearby.

His earlier books include:

> *The Justice Diary*, a reflection on his years working in the criminal justice system and his turn toward healing and accountability.
>
> *A Third Half Journal*, chronicling the inward turn that often comes in life's second act and the emergence of something entirely new.
>
> *Walt's Last Year*, a novel imagining Walt Whitman's final journey through the modern world, guided by poetry, memory, and love.
>
> *What I Remember*, a personal memoir of early life, family, and the deeper threads that weave beneath memory's surface.

Travels With Pa began as a blog during Fred's six-month journey around the world and evolved into a meditation on solitude, friendship, and the delicate art of presence. Through journal entries, vignettes, and chance encounters, Fred invites the reader to see travel not as escape, but as a return - to simplicity, to wonder, and to the quietly enduring self.

Fred continues to write, explore, and wonder aloud - often with a cup of tea in hand and a grandchild beside him.

Pa (left) & Fred (right)

www.ingramcontent.com/pod-product-compliance
Lightning Source LLC
Chambersburg PA
CBHW071150070526
44584CB00019B/2733